THE BRO
SOFT FRUIT
RECIPE BOOK

COMPILED & PUBLISHED BY
GEERINGS OF ASHFORD LTD

Illustrations by Barbara Seth

ISBN 1 873953 22 4

Designed and printed by Geerings of Ashford Limited
Cobbs Wood House, Chart Road, Ashford, Kent TN23 1EP

CONTENTS

BROGDALE SOFT FRUIT

If you were to make a list of all the things that have come to represent the British summer, the chances are that the sound of willow on leather, the smell of freshly mown grass and the sweet luxury of strawberries and cream would be close to the top.

The strawberry has, like a number of other foods, attained a rare, elevated status. Even in these days of year-round availability and sometimes indifferent flavour, it retains a certain mystique. The strawberry symbolises refinement and elegance, good times and good taste.

Yet while the strawberry may be the most obvious example of a fruit which has come to represent the easy living of the summer season and early autumn, the berries and currants featured in this collection of recipes also have an important and, some would say, underestimated role in our culinary heritage.

Just as each group of soft fruits has its own character in the kitchen, each has its own fascinating history. The notes which follow provide an introduction to each group and trace their development.

STRAWBERRY

The strawberry may be the soft fruit which most readily brings to mind balmy, carefree summer days, but the fruit we know and enjoy today is, in fact, the result of a good deal of good luck.

The small but flavoursome, wild wood strawberry has been savoured from the very earliest times. Literary evidence indicates that they were known to both the

Greeks and Romans but it wasn't until the late 14th Century that cultivation began in earnest in Europe with 1,200 plants grown in the Royal Gardens of Charles V at The Louvre in Paris.

In 1545, the writer Estinne noted that strawberries were a delicacy served with sugar and cream or wine and that the berries were the size of a hazelnut.

Around about the same time one Andrew Boorde also drew attention to the flavour of the strawberry by writing that "raw crayme, undecoted, eaten with strawberries... is a rural man's "blanket." Some things never change!

It is not only in its effect on the taste buds that the strawberry is unlike any other fruit. It is also biologically different. The plump, fleshy part of the strawberry we treasure isn't the fruit of the plant at all. Instead it is the seeds - uniquely on the outside - which are the fruit.

The strawberry is from the family Fragaria - a root derived from its fragrance and still evident in its French name, Fraise, and the Italian Fragola. The roots of the English name are less clear. While one school of thought concludes that it derives from the straw used to protect plants against the extremes of climate, a second insists that it has developed from Straberry, thanks to its habit of growing out along the ground in any and all directions.

While gastronomic fashion has dictated that interest in the small wild strawberries has been renewed in recent times, the strawberry which most know and love has developed not from Europe but North and South America.

As the New World was gradually opened up, pioneers discovered F. Virginiana, North America's native strawberry. They also encountered another species, F. Chiloensis which grew widely but - as the name suggests - was particularly associated with Chile.

First Virginiana and then Chiloensis were introduced to Europe and while neither variety was outstanding in its own right, the cross, F. Ananassa, was the true forebear of today's strawberry.

Now there are simply hundreds of strawberry varieties, each with its own characteristics. Whichever variety you choose for the kitchen you should look for plump fruit with green tops. Strawberries are best when they are perfectly ripe so any stains on the punnet suggest that the fruit is past its best.

RASPBERRIES

Those who adore the distinctive penetrating taste of the Raspberry may be surprised to know that the Greeks and Romans, so perceptive in other areas, chose not to eat them at all. Instead, they were used medically, with the blossom being mixed with honey to make an eye ointment.

It was left to later civilisations to realise the full potential of the raspberry which grows wild throughout the cooler parts of the Northern hemisphere from north of the Arctic Circle to Western and Northern Asia.

While the botanical name for the raspberry is Ridaeus, the English word rather more prosaic. Although the deriviation is not completely clear, it is thought to come from the Old English 'Raspis' which refers to the fruit's rasping surface.

Many Raspberry lovers believe the only way to eat the fruit is fresh, with cream or ice cream. Indeed, its consistency makes it unsuitable for many culinary purposes and raspberries are often featured in menus as syrups and sauces rather than the principal ingredient of a main dish.

GOOSEBERRY

It may be not the most fashionable of fruits in the late 20th century, but the humble Gooseberry was once so popular that enthusiasts formed clubs to appreciate its taste and develop new varieties.

Perhaps it is the name itself which has earned the Gooseberry such a bad press. After all, its use as a description of the awkward outsider at a meeting of lovers hardly makes one feel comfortable, while its veiny and hairy exterior make it an object of particular mirth among children.

Remember the joke: *Q. What's Green and goes up and down?*
A. A Goosegog in a lift.

But does the Gooseberry deserve to be the butt of infant humour? Probably not. In the kitchen it is a star performer in pies, crumbles, tarts, fools and jams while enthusiasts rave about the distinctive flavours of dessert gooseberries.

As with many other fruit, opinion is divided as to how the Gooseberry got its name. While some opine that it derives from the similarity between the Gooseberry bush and the Gorse, others - more interestingly - believe it comes from the traditional use of the fruit to make a sauce to accompany Goose.

In France the Gooseberry is known as Groseille Marquereau, or Mackrel Currant and is served as a sauce with fish.

While nobody can claim to know how the Gooseberry got its name we can be certain that the fruit grows wild in most of the northern temperate zone and flourishes in cool, moist or high regions.

Among the first known references to Gooseberries in Britain, is a fruiterers bill dating from 1276 which shows bushes - probably from France - had been supplied to the Court of King Edward I.

Gooseberries enjoyed their heyday during Victorian times when amateur clubs in the North or Midlands of England competed furiously amongst one another to achieve the biggest fruit and the best flavour.

The Eston Bridge Old Gooseberry Society in Yorkshire was founded in 1800 and has held annual competitions - war permitting - ever since.

THE BLACKBERRY AND OTHER BERRIES

There are some 2000 varieties of Blackberry grown throughout the cooler parts of the world and few have grown up in Britain without discovering the delights of picking the fruit growing wild in the hedgerows in early autumn.

While the British tend to treasure the versatile Blackberry rather as the legitimate bounty of a Sunday afternoon ramble along country lanes, it is commercially grown in both Europe and the USA.

The Blackberry is of the same genus - Rubus - as the Raspberry and the similarity of shape, size, leaves and thorns can make it difficult to tell the two apart.

Today the development of hybrids means that the Blackberry has a number of close relatives, the best known of which are the Loganberry - named after one Judge Logan of Santa Cruz, California, and the increasingly popular Tayberry which has large, dark red fruit.

CURRANT AFFAIRS

Clever marketing over the years meant that most of us know something of the properties of the blackcurrant. They are, for example, a rich source of Vitamin C with just half a dozen black currants containing more of the Vitamin than a whole lemon.

Indeed, it was the medicinal properties rather than culinary potential of the black currant which first brought it to prominence. For years it remained in the shadow of the red currant whose flavour was widely appreciated in Northern Europe where they are still used in desserts, sauces, jellies and even soups.

One authoritative reference goes as far as to suggest that blackcurrants were generally reviled from around the 16th century when the redcurrant was at the height of its popularity.

But then the tide turned. Today the blackcurrant holds sway. It is loved for its juice and to add a distinct sharp flavour to jams, sorbets and a range of other desserts. Mechanical harvesting techniques mean the blackurrant is grown commercially, largely for its juice, in Britain, Russia and other northern countries although to this day the Americans remain strangely resistant to its charms.

One must not, of course, forget the third type of currant, the whitecurrant. Botanically they are a variety of the redcurrant although they are less acid and considered rather more refined. In recipes, red and whitecurrants can often be combined.

Fruit Desserts

BLACKBERRIES IN LEMON CREAM (serves 4)

4 eggs (separated)
6ozs/175g sugar
5tbsp/90ml lemon juice
1tsp grated lemon rind
½ pint/300ml double cream
Fresh blackberries

Beat the yolks in a mixing bowl until thick and then beat in the lemon juice, rind and sugar. Gently heat using a double saucepan, stirring constantly until the mixture thickens. Leave aside to cool. Whisk one of the egg whites until stiff and fold into the mixture, then add the cream and fruit. Pour into serving dishes and garnish with berries. Chill in the refrigerator for 3 hours.

HIGHLAND DESSERT

4ozs/120g rolled oats
½ pint/300ml milk
1 grated apple
2ozs/50g chopped hazelnuts
Juice of 1 orange
Juice of 1 lemon
1 orange, peeled and broken into segments
1 banana (sliced)
2ozs/50g fresh pineapple (sliced)
Honey or sugar
¼ pint/150ml double cream
2ozs/50g blackberries
A few raspberries

Soak overnight the rolled oats and the milk. Then add the apple, hazelnuts, juice of the orange and lemon, the orange segments, banana and pineapple. Add honey or sugar to taste and mix thoroughly. Garnish each portion with the cream, blackberries and raspberries

ORANGE AND RASPBERRY COMPOTE

4ozs/125g sugar
20fl.ozs/600ml water
5fl.ozs/150ml Grand Marnier
12 oranges (peeled)
1lb/450g raspberries
Natural yoghurt

Add the sugar and water in a saucepan, stirring over a low heat until the sugar is dissolved. Bring slowly to the boil, cook for 2-3 minutes and then remove to cool. Add the Grand Marnier, stirring gently. Cut the oranges into slices, removing the pips. Place the orange slices and raspberries into the serving dish and pour over the prepared liquid. Cover the compote and place in the refrigerator for 12 hours. This dessert is delicious on its own or with natural yoghurt.

COMPOTE OF CURRANTS WITH CREME FRAICHE

12ozs/350g sugar
20fl.ozs/600ml water
1lb/450g fresh currants (red, white or black)
Creme fraiche

Prepare the syrup by adding the sugar to the water in a saucepan, place over a low heat until the sugar is dissolved and then bring to the boil for 2-3 minutes. Place the prepared currants into the boiling syrup and bring back to the boil for a few minutes. Remove from heat and leave aside to cool. Place the compote in the serving dish, cover and refrigerate for at least 12 hours. Serve the compote with creme fraiche.

RED CURRANTS WITH RED WINE

1lb/450g red currants
5ozs/150g castor sugar
1/2 pint/300ml red wine

Remove the stems and blossom ends from the fruit and put in a glass dish, sprinkle over with the castor sugar. Pour over the red wine and leave to stand in a cool place for 1 hour.

GOOSEBERRY COMPOTE

2lbs/1kg gooseberries
8ozs/250g white sugar
1pint/600ml water
1 small wine glass of Kirsch
1 tbsp apricot jam

Place prepared gooseberries into boiling water for 2 minutes, remove and drain thoroughly. Put the sugar and water in a pan, bring to the boil and cook for 10 minutes. Add the gooseberries, Kirsch and apricot jam. Continue to simmer until gooseberries are cooked. Leave to cool and serve.

SUMMER FRUITS WITH RASPBERRY SAUCE (serves 4)

1lb/450g mixture of raspberries, blackcurrants, blackberries and strawberries
8ozs/225g fresh raspberries
1oz/25g sugar

Purée the raspberries using a blender. To remove the pips press the liquid through a kitchen sieve into a bowl, then stir in the sugar ensuring that it is dissolved. Place the mixture in the refrigerator for at least 2 hours before serving. Clean and de-stalk the fresh summer fruits. Place the fruits into individual serving dishes and pour the chilled raspberry sauce over the fruit.

TIPSY FRUIT CUP (serves 8-10)

5ozs/150g dried apricots
12ozs/350g mixed dried fruit
1lb/500g fresh cherries
1 grapefruit (peeled and segmented)
4ozs/125g preserved kumquats
1lb/500g figs in syrup
3 bananas (sliced)
Strawberries, raspberries or any other seasonal soft fruits
Juice of 1 lemon
Sugar to taste
½ a glass of cognac

Place the dried apricots and mixed dried fruit into a saucepan with sufficient water to cover, bring to the boil and simmer until tender, covering the saucepan. Remove from the heat to cool, then dice the cooked dried fruit. Add the rest of the ingredients to the mixture and mix in a large bowl. Leave overnight to mature. Serve chilled with sponge finger biscuits.

HIGHLAND FLING TRIFLE

8 trifle sponges
2tbsp raspberry jam
8ozs/250g fresh summer fruits of your choice
¼ pint/150ml mixture in equal quantities of Scotch whisky, Drambuie and green ginger wine
6 egg yolks
2ozs/50g castor sugar
½ ounce/13g cornflour
½ pint/300ml milk
1pt/600ml double cream
1 large banana (sliced)
1tbsp/15ml Scotch whisky
Glacé cherries and toasted almonds to decorate

Break the trifle sponges into small pieces, mix with the raspberry jam and place in the trifle dish. Add the summer fruits and the alcoholic mix and leave aside for an hour. Carefully blend the egg yolks, cornflour and sugar in a bowl. Place the milk and half the cream in a saucepan and gently heat, but do not allow to boil. Pour into the egg mixture continuously stirring and pour back into the saucepan. Over a gentle heat stir until it thickens, then remove from heat to cool. Cover the sponge and summer fruit mix with the sliced banana, then pour the mixture from the saucepan over the bananas. Whip the rest of the cream with a little whisky and sugar and spread over the trifle, decorating with the glacé cherries and almonds.

FRUIT DREAM

8ozs/250g strawberries
8ozs/250g raspberries
1 mango
4tbsp/60ml Kirsch
Sugar to taste

For the sauce -
3 egg yolks
1½ tbsp/25ml Kirsch
1 tsp lemon juice
1tsp grated lemon rind
4fl.oz/125ml double cream (whipped)

Peel and dice the mango, slice the strawberries and mix with the raspberries. Place the fruit mixture into a flameproof dish and sprinkle with the Kirsch and sugar. Place in a refrigerator for at least 3 hours.

To make the sauce beat the egg yolks and sugar carefully, heating gently using a double saucepan until the mix is thick and creamy. Add the Kirsch, lemon juice and rind, beating continuously and fold in the cream. Pour this over the marinated fruit and place under a hot grill for a few minutes until golden brown. Serve hot.

SUMMER FRUIT COMPOTE

8ozs/250g sugar
½ pint/300ml water
1lb/500g blackcurrants
Grated rind and juice of ½ an orange
4ozs/125g strawberries
4ozs/125g blackberries
8ozs/250g raspberries
1tbsp/15ml arrowroot
2tbsp/30ml port

Create the syrup mix by placing the sugar and water into a saucepan, heating gently until dissolved. Boil the syrup for 2-3 minutes and then add the blackcurrants and grated orange rind. Reduce the heat and simmer for 20 minutes or until the fruit is soft. Pour the mixture through a sieve retaining the syrup in a bowl. Place the strained blackcurrants in the serving dish, adding the remaining fruit. Pour the syrup mix into the saucepan and bring to the boil. Mix the arrowroot with the orange juice and carefully add to the boiling syrup. Continue to cook, stirring continuously, until the mixture is thickened and clear. Mix in the port and immediately pour over the fruits. Leave for a few hours to cool before serving.

DANISH DELIGHT

1lb/500g redcurrants
8ozs/250g raspberries
2ozs/50g blackcurrants
2ozs/50g sago

Place fruit in a pan and add sufficient water to cover the bottom of the pan. Bring to the boil and cook gently until the fruit is soft. Strain cooked fruit through a sieve and use a little of the liquid to blend with the sago. Bring the remaining liquid back to the boil and add the blended sago, stir thoroughly for 2 minutes. Remove the pan from the heat and continue to stir the mixture while it cools. Pour into individual glasses and serve with cream and sugar.

BERRY TOT (serves 6)

8ozs/250g tinned blackcurrants in syrup (drained)
3ozs/100g castor sugar
8ozs/250g fresh raspberries
8ozs/250g fresh strawberries
4tbsp/60ml Scotch whisky

Mix the blackcurrants with the fresh raspberries and strawberries and sprinkle with the whisky and 1oz/25g sugar. Bring the drained syrup juice and remaining sugar to the boil, ensuring that the sugar is dissolved and pour over the fruit. Leave aside to cool and then place in the refrigerator for 2-3 hours. It is delicious served with natural yoghurt, creme fraiche or vanilla ice cream.

SALAD OF SUMMER FRUITS

Selection of fresh summer soft fruits
Sugar
Sherry or white wine (whatever your taste) or
Whipped double cream

Prepare the fruit and place in a serving dish in layers, each layer sprinkled generously with sugar. Set aside to chill. Just prior to serving, pour over the sherry or white wine or cover with whipped double cream. The fruit should be stirred gently when serving.

RASPBERRIES IN MELBA SAUCE (*serves 4*)

1lb/500g raspberries
2ozs/50g icing sugar

Place 4ozs/125g raspberries in a sieve and press through. Gradually add the icing sugar to the purée. Prepare the remaining fresh raspberries and place them into individual serving dishes. Pour the sauce over the raspberries. Best left for a few hours before serving.

APRICOT BASKET WITH STRAWBERRIES

9 good apricots
7ozs/200g wild strawberries
2ozs/50g castor sugar
½ pint/300ml fresh cream

Halve and stone the apricots. Whisk the cream until it is firm, spoon half of it into the centre of a glass dish and place the apricot halves around the edge. Fill each half up with the wild strawberries and put a little cream on top of each one.

RASPBERRY WHIP

12ozs/350g raspberries
8ozs/250g castor sugar
1 egg white

Beat all the ingredients together and serve either on slices of sponge cake or piled into individual serving dishes.

STRAWBERRY PINEAPPLE COCKTAIL (serves 4)

8ozs/250g fresh strawberries
4 pineapple rings (sliced)
12tbsp/180ml orange juice
2tbsp/30ml lemon juice
Angelica to decorate

Put aside 6/8 strawberries for decoration. Slice the remaining strawberries and mix with the pineapple. Mix the orange and lemon juices and place in the refrigerator to chill. Place the fruit in the serving dishes and pour over the chilled juice mix. Use the reserved strawberries and angelica to decorate.

STRAWBERRIES FLAMBÉ (serves 6-8)

2lbs/1kg strawberries
Peel of 1 lemon
Juice and peel of 2 oranges
2ozs/50g sugar
4fl.ozs/150ml brandy

Prepare the strawberries and arrange in flameproof serving dish. Put the lemon peel, orange juice and peel and sugar in a pan and cook slowly, pressing the peel with a spoon to extract as much flavour as possible. Discard the peel and spoon the hot syrup over the fruit. Pour over the brandy and light. Serve immediately with fresh double cream or vanilla ice cream.

WILD STRAWBERRIES WITH LEMON

1lb/500g strawberries
6ozs/350g castor sugar
Juice of 1 large or 2 small lemons

Wash and hull the strawberries. Place a layer of strawberries in the serving dish, followed by a layer of sugar. Repeat with another layer of fruit followed by a layer of sugar until the fruit is used up. Pour the lemon juice over the fruit. Shake the dish gently without bruising the fruit. Set aside for an hour or two to allow the juices to mix before serving.

STRAWBERRIES WITH RED WINE

1lb/500g strawberries
7ozs/375g castor sugar
1 glass red wine

Wash and hull the strawberries, cutting any large strawberries in half. In a serving dish arrange alternate layers of strawberries and sugar until all the fruit is used. Pour over the wine, shaking the dish gently to mix the wine. Leave to stand for an hour before serving.

GOURMET STRAWBERRIES (serves 4)

1lb/500g strawberries (hulled and washed)
Juice of 1 lemon
Sugar to taste

Using about 4ozs/125g of the strawberries purée in a food processor with the lemon juice and sugar. Taste for sweetness. Put the remaining strawberries in one large or four individual serving dishes and spoon the purée over the top. Leave to chill for about an hour before serving with or without cream.

STRAWBERRY MALLOW (serves 4-6)

½ pint/300ml thick cream
8ozs/250g small marshmallows or large ones cut up
1lb/500g sliced fresh strawberries
4tbsp/60ml sherry or rum

Whip the cream until firm, fold in the marshmallows and add the strawberries. Spoon into individual serving dishes and pour over the sherry or rum.

Soufflés, Mousses & Jellies

BLACKBERRY MOUSSE

1lb/500g blackberries
1oz/25g castor sugar
3 eggs
3ozs/75g castor sugar
½ ounce/13g gelatine
Juice of ½ a lemon
2tbsp/30ml water
¼ pint/150ml double cream

To decorate -
3-4fl.oz/90-120ml double cream
Castor sugar to sweeten

Gently cook the washed blackberries in a saucepan with 1oz/25g of sugar until soft. Strain them through a kitchen sieve and leave the resultant purée to cool. Beat the eggs and 3ozs/75g sugar in a basin over a pan of hot water continuing to beat until the bowl is cold and the mixture is such that it holds its shape. Place the gelatine in the mixture of lemon juice and water and dissolve it over a gentle heat. Carefully whip the cream to a stiff consistency.

Add 6fl.oz/200ml of the blackberry purée to the egg and sugar mixture and then add the dissolved gelatine and cream. Fold the mixtures together quickly but lightly. Place the bowl on some ice and continue to stir the mixture until it thickens. Pour into a serving dish and leave for 1-2 hours to set. Just before serving, spoon the remaining purée over the mousse. Whip the remaining cream and sugar and use to decorate.

CRUNCHY BLACKBERRY WHIP (serves 4-6)

8ozs/250g ginger biscuits
2ozs/50g butter (melted)
1lb/500g blackberries
4ozs/100g sugar
1/4 pint/150ml apple purée
1 small can evaporated milk
Half ounce/13g gelatine
2tbsp/30ml hot water

Using a blender, break the ginger biscuits into fine pieces. Thoroughly mix the biscuit crumbs with the melted butter and press the resultant mixture onto the bottom and sides of a pie dish. Put in a cool place to set.

Place the blackberries and half the sugar into a saucepan and heat until the fruit is soft. Mash into a smooth mixture and stir in the apple purée. Whisk the evaporated milk until stiff and fold into the fruit mix. Place the gelatine in the hot water and encourage it to dissolve over a little heat. When cooled, mix in with the fruit, add the rest of the sugar and pour onto the ginger biscuit base. Once it is set, decorate with whipped cream.

BLACKBERRY MOUSSE (serves 4-6)

1/2 ounce/13g powdered gelatine
Grated rind and juice of 1 lemon
1lb/500g blackberries
1oz/25g castor sugar
5fl.oz/150ml natural yoghurt

To decorate -
Extra blackberries and mint sprigs
Icing sugar to dust (if desired)

Place the lemon juice in a bowl, sprinkle with the gelatine powder and leave to soak. In a saucepan, stew the blackberries with the sugar, lemon rind and a dash of water, heating gently and simmer for about 10 minutes or until the fruit is soft. Remove from the heat and leave to cool. Pour the mixture into a glass measuring jug, it should make 16fl.oz/450ml. If it is a little less, add water to make up to this quantity. Combine the fruit mixture, the yoghurt and the gelatine in a bowl, stirring continuously. Pour into individual serving dishes and chill for a few hours before serving. Garnish with whole blackberries and mint sprigs and dust with icing sugar if desired.

BLACKBERRY AND APPLE SHAPE

1lb/500g blackberries
4ozs/100g sugar
2 cloves
1lb/500g apples (peeled, cored and sliced)
½ ounce/13g gelatine
Lemon peel
6fl.ozs/450ml whipped cream

Cook apples and blackberries together, add the sugar, lemon rind and cloves. When soft and pulpy, strain through a sieve. Dissolve the gelatine in a little hot water and add to the purée. Spoon the mixture around the edge of the serving bowl and fill the centre with the cream.

CURRANT SOUFFLÉ

1lb/500g mixed black, red and white currants
2ozs/50g granulated sugar
¼ pint/150ml cold water
4 large eggs
6ozs/150g castor sugar
½ pint/300ml lightly whipped double cream
½ ounce/13g powdered gelatine
3tbsp/45ml warm water

Prepare the currants and put in a pan with the granulated sugar and cold water. Heat slowly until the sugar is dissolved and then simmer until the fruit is soft. Press the cooked fruit through a sieve to remove the pips and make a purée. Whisk the eggs and castor sugar together in a large bowl until light and fluffy, fold in the currant purée and then the cream. Dissolve the gelatine in the warm water over a very gentle heat. When fully dissolved, add to the fruit mixture.

Prepare a 6"/15cm soufflé dish with a "collar" of greaseproof paper about 2"/5cm higher than the edge of the dish and secured with sellotape. When the mixture is on the point of setting, pour into the soufflé dish and leave it to set in a cool place. When ready to serve, carefully peel away the paper collar and decorate as desired. Serve immediately.

RED CURRANT MOUSSE

1lb/500g red currants
7ozs/200g castor sugar
1/2 pint/300ml fresh cream

Remove the stems and blossom ends of the currants, crush the fruit with a fork and press through a sieve. Add the sugar and mix thoroughly. Whip the cream until very thick and add to the fruit mixture. Put in a serving dish and leave in a refrigerator to set.

BLACKCURRANT MERINGUE

2 egg whites
4ozs/125g castor sugar
4ozs/125g granulated sugar
1/4 pint/150ml water
1lb/500g blackcurrants
3/4 ounce/20g gelatine
4tbsp/60ml cold water
1/4 pint/150ml double cream
1 tsp grated chocolate

Set oven at 150C/300F/Gas Mark 2.

To make the meringue, whisk the egg whites until stiff and then add half the sugar, continuing to whisk. Fold in the rest of the sugar. Using a piping kit, pipe small mounds of meringue on to baking paper. Bake in a preheated oven for about one and a half hours.

Create a syrup mix by gently heating the sugar and water in a saucepan until dissolved. Add the prepared fruit and continue to cook gently for approximately 15 minutes until the fruit is soft. Press fruit mix through a sieve. Dissolve the gelatine in water over a gentle heat. In a bowl, mix this with the purée and leave to cool, stirring occasionally. Pour the mixture into a soufflé dish and place in a refrigerator to set. Turn out onto a serving dish. Cover with the thickly whipped double cream and place the meringues on top. This dish is improved by sprinkling with grated chocolate.

GOOSEBERRY MOUSSE

GOOSEBERRY MOUSSE (serves 4)

½ ounce/13g powdered gelatine
4tbsp/60ml cold water
1lb/500g gooseberries
2oz/50g castor sugar
5fl.oz/150ml natural yoghurt
A few drops of green food colouring (if desired)
Mint sprigs to decorate

Put the gelatine and cold water in a small bowl and leave to dissolve. Put the prepared gooseberries in a saucepan with 2tbsp/30ml cold water, bring to the boil, reduce the heat and leave to simmer for about 15 minutes or until the fruit is tender. Take out any excess juice and reserve. Stir in the dissolved gelatine, stirring thoroughly, and leave mixture to cool slightly.

Put the gooseberries and sugar in a food processor and process to make a purée. Pass the purée through a sieve to remove all the pips and put into a measuring jug. Measure the quantity and make up to 16fl.ozs/450ml with the reserved juice. When the mixture is beginning to set, fold in the yoghurt and add a few drops of green colouring if desired. Pour the mousse into a large serving dish or individual dishes and put into a refrigerator to set. Decorate with sprigs of mint to serve.

GOOSEBERRY SOUFFLÉ

1lb/500g gooseberries
¼ pint/150ml water
4ozs/125g granulated sugar
4 eggs (separated)
2ozs/50g castor sugar
¼ pint/150ml double cream
½ ounce/13g gelatine
5tbsp/75ml water

To decorate -
7fl.oz/200ml double cream
Finely chopped browned almonds

To make the purée put the prepared gooseberries, water and sugar in a pan, bring to the boil and simmer until the fruit is soft. Allow to cool slightly and then put fruit through a sieve. This should leave about half a pint/300ml of purée. Prepare soufflé dish.

Put the egg yolks, castor sugar and purée into a bowl, place bowl in a pan of hot water and whisk mixture until it begins to thicken. Remove bowl and continue to whisk until it is cool. Lightly whip the cream and stir into the gooseberry mixture. Soak the gelatine in the water and dissolve over a gentle heat and stir into the soufflé mix. When it begins to thicken, fold in the firmly whipped egg whites with a metal spoon. Turn the mixture into the soufflé dish and leave to set. When ready to serve, decorate with whipped double cream and the nuts.

RASPBERRY AND REDCURRANT MOULD (serves 4-6)

1lb/500g raspberries
8ozs/250g redcurrants
12ozs/375g granulated sugar
½ pint/300ml water
Gelatine
¼ pint/150ml whipped double cream

Prepare a ring mould about 1½-2pt/900-1200ml capacity.

Put the raspberries and redcurrants in a saucepan with the sugar and water and stir over a gentle heat until the sugar is dissolved. Leave to cool slightly. Rub cooked fruit through a sieve and measure resultant purée. (For each pint/600ml of purée allow ¾ oz/20g gelatine). Soak the gelatine in a little water allowing 3 tbsp/45ml water to every 20g gelatine. When dissolved, add to the warmed fruit purée and stir until completely absorbed.
Pour into the wetted ring mould and leave to set in a cool place.
When ready to serve, turn out of mould and serve with the cream piled in the centre.

SUMMER FRUIT TERRINE (serves 6)

2½ozs/65g castor sugar
9fl.oz/250ml water
9fl.oz/250ml white wine
3tbsp/45ml lemon juice
¾ oz/20g powdered gelatine
4tbsp/60ml water
8ozs/250g redcurrants
8ozs/250g strawberries
Fresh mint sprigs

Put the sugar and water in a pan, place over a gentle heat to dissolve sugar, bring to the boil and allow to bubble for one minute. Pour into a bowl, leave to cool and then add the wine and lemon juice, blending thoroughly. Sprinkle the gelatine over the 60ml of water, leave for 5 minutes and then place bowl over a pan of simmering water. Heat gently until dissolved and set aside to cool. Pour into the syrup.

Prepare the redcurrants and slice strawberries about ¼-inch/6mm thick. Put a non-stick loaf tin (2pt/1.2lt) in a roasting tin surrounded with ice cubes and top up with enough cold water to come halfway up the side of the tin. Put a thin layer of redcurrants on the bottom of the tin and spoon over enough jelly liquid to cover. Leave to set. Layer the remaining fruit in the tin and spoon over the jelly to fill. Leave in the ice cubes until jelly begins to set and then put in a refrigerator for at least three hours to completely set.

To serve, turn out the jelly onto a serving dish and decorate with mint sprigs and a few redcurrants.

CHERRY AND RASPBERRY JELLY

8ozs/250g cherries
1lb/500g raspberries
8ozs/250g red or black currants
1pint/600ml water
2ozs/50g fine sago
4-6ozs/100-150g granulated sugar
Clotted cream to serve

De-stalk and wash the fruit. De-stone the cherries and crack the kernels. Stew the fruit and cracked kernels with the water in a covered saucepan for approximately 15 minutes until the fruit is soft. Strain the fruit through a kitchen sieve. Pour the mixture back into the saucepan and add the sago and sugar to taste. Bring to the boil and cook carefully for a further 4-5 minutes stirring consistently. Pour into a wetted mould and leave to cool. Turn out to serve.

SMALL RASPBERRY SOUFFLÉS

1lb/500g raspberries
4ozs/100g sweet almonds
7ozs/200g icing sugar
White of 1 egg
25 small paper moulds

Set the oven at 250F/130C/Gas Mark $\frac{1}{2}$

Put the almonds through a food processor or grinder until very fine and then mix with the sugar. Beat the egg white until it is firm and sprinkle it on the almond and sugar mix and stir in lightly. Put the paper moulds on a baking tin and put one or two raspberries in each, drop a little of the cream on top and sprinkle with icing sugar. Put in a very slow oven until they become quite firm.

As an alternative you can use strawberries for this recipe selecting 25 good sound fruit.

RASPBERRY RING (serves 4)

8ozs/250g raspberries
A little sugar
A little water
1 raspberry flavoured jelly
½ pint/300ml cream or whipped evaporated milk
2-3 meringue cases
8ozs/250g whole raspberries
A little castor sugar

Rinse out a ring mould which holds approximately 1pint/600ml. Create a mash with the raspberries, a little sugar and enough water to give 1pint/600ml. Add the jelly to the raspberry mix and heat until the jelly is dissolved. Pour into the wet ring mould and turn out when set. Whip the cream to a firm consistency and whisk in a little sugar. Break up the meringue cases, fold them into the cream and add in a few raspberries. Pour the mixture into the centre of the jelly ring. Ready to serve.

STRAWBERRIES IN JELLY

1lb/500g strawberries
4ozs/125g sugar
4tbsp/60ml brandy
2 strawberry jellies (made up with 1pt/600ml water plus ¼ pint/150ml claret or red wine)
2pt/1200ml jelly mould

Hull the strawberries and soak in the sugar and brandy. Make up the jelly and when nearly cold, pour into the mould sufficient to cover the bottom. Allow to almost set and then put a layer of strawberries; continue with the layers finishing with a layer of jelly. Put in a refrigerator to set and turn out when ready to serve.

Try using raspberries with raspberry jelly as an alternative.

COLD RASPBERRY OR STRAWBERRY SOUFFLÉ

8ozs/250g raspberries or strawberries
1tbsp red currant jelly
4 eggs
3/4 pint/450ml milk
2ozs/50g sugar
1oz/25g cornflour
1 liqueur glass of maraschino
2ozs/50g butter
Vanilla flavouring
1/2 ounce/13g gelatine dissolved in a little hot water

Mix the cornflour with a little of the cold milk. Put the remaining milk in a saucepan, add the vanilla, sugar and moistened cornflour and stirring continuously bring to the boil and simmer until the mixture thickens. Remove from heat. Rub the strawberries through a sieve and stir the purée into the cornflour mix. Stirring all the time, add the butter, egg yolks and cream and whisk over a very gentle heat until the eggs are set. Add the red currant jelly to the dissolved gelatine and strain into the thickened mixture stirring thoroughly. Whip the egg whites until very firm and carefully fold into the mixture, finally adding the maraschino. Pour into a papered soufflé dish, dissolve a little red currant jelly and when nearly cold pour over the top. Place soufflé in a refrigerator to set and remove paper before serving.

STRAWBERRY CHARLOTTE

8ozs/250g strawberries
1oz/25g castor sugar
A little water
3 eggs
2 egg yolks
6ozs/175g castor sugar
1/2 pint/300ml double cream
1/2 ounce/13g gelatine
Juice of 1/2 a lemon with 5tbsp/150ml water
To decorate -
1/4 pint/150ml double cream
Fine sponge fingers
Angelica

Press the strawberries through a sieve and add the 1oz/25g of sugar and a little water to make the purée. Put the eggs, yolks and castor sugar in a bowl and whisk until the mixture is thick and frothy. Lightly whip the cream and dissolve the gelatine over a low heat in the lemon juice and water. Add the purée, gelatine and cream to the mousse in a bowl standing in ice and continue to stir until the mixture becomes creamy and thick. Pour into a cake tin lined with foil and put in a refrigerator to set. When ready to serve remove very carefully onto a serving dish. Whip the cream, spread on the sponge fingers and press them overlapping around the charlotte. Decorate the top with piped cream and angelica. Serve immediately.

QUICK STRAWBERRY AND BANANA MERINGUE (serves 4)

6 bananas
8ozs/250g strawberries
A little orange or pineapple juice
1x6"/150cm meringue case

Reserve half a banana (dipped in the fruit juice to prevent it browning) and a few strawberries for decoration.

Mash the remaining bananas and strawberries with the fruit juice. Fill the flan case with the fruit mixture and chill thoroughly. When ready to serve, decorate with the reserved banana and strawberries.

STRAWBERRY CHEESE RING (serves 4)

1lb/500g strawberries
8oz/250g cottage cheese
2ozs/50g castor sugar
Juice of 1 medium orange
1 sachet gelatine
2 kiwi fruit

Using half the strawberries place in a food processor or liquidiser with the cottage cheese and the sugar (reserving a teaspoon of sugar), and purée. Put the orange juice in a small bowl and sprinkle over the gelatine. Stand bowl in simmering water and leave while the gelatine dissolves and then add to the purée, mixing thoroughly. Pour the mixture into a 1½pt/900ml ring mould and place in a refrigerator to set.

When ready to serve, dip the mould briefly in hot water and then turn out ring on a serving dish. Halve or slice the remaining strawberries, peel and slice the kiwi fruit and arrange in the centre of the ring. Sprinkle over the remaining sugar. Serve immediately.

QUICK STRAWBERRY MOUSSE

8ozs/250g strawberries
6ozs/175g castor sugar
½ pint/300ml fresh double cream

Press the strawberries through a sieve. Whip the cream until firm, add the sugar and puréed strawberries and mix thoroughly. Pour into a glass serving dish and leave in a cool place until ready to serve.

STRAWBERRY INDULGENCE (serves 6-8)

12ozs/350g strawberries
½ ounce/13g gelatine
4tbsp/60ml water
16fl.oz/450ml carton of custard sauce
½ pint/300ml whipped cream

For the sauce -
8ozs/250g strawberrries
2ozs/50g castor sugar
1tbsp/15ml raspberry flavoured liqueur (if desired)

Reserve a few strawberries to use for decoration and press the remainder through a sieve to purée. Dissolve the gelatine in the water over a gentle heat. Pour the custard into a bowl, stir in the dissolved gelatine and set aside to cool, stirring occasionally to prevent a skin forming. Stir in the strawberry purée and then gently fold in the whipped cream. Pour the mixture into a mould and chill until set.

To make the sauce, slice the strawberries into a bowl, sprinkle with the sugar and liqueur (if using), cover and leave to stand for about an hour. Then press through a sieve to form a purée, pour into a small jug and chill.

Place the mould briefly in hot water before turning out on to a serving dish. Decorate with the reserved strawberries and serve with the chilled sauce.

Creams, Fools & Custards

BLACKBERRY FOOL (serves 4)

1lb/500g blackberries
1pt/600ml double cream
Castor sugar to taste

Place the blackberries in a saucepan, add sufficient water just to cover and cook until soft. Add sugar to taste. Press the cooked blackberries through a sieve and stir the purée into the whipped cream. Serve cold in individual glasses with wafers or sponge finger biscuits.

BLACKBERRY DELIGHT

8ozs/250g blackberries
1/4 ounce/12g powdered gelatine
Juice and grated zest of 1 lemon
1/2 pint/300ml double cream
4ozs/125g castor sugar

To decorate -
Whipped cream

Prepare the blackberries and reserve a few for decoration. Put the gelatine and lemon juice in a small pan and heat gently until dissolved. Allow to cool. Whisk the cream until stiff, add the blackberries, sugar and lemon zest and mix thoroughly. Add the dissolved gelatine and stir well. Pour mixture into a wetted mould and place in a refrigerator to set. When ready to serve, turn out and decorate with the whipped cream and reserved blackberries.

TIPSY REDCURRANT DESSERT (serves 4)

12ozs/450g ripe red currants
12ozs/450g cream cheese
2ozs/50g castor sugar
2-3 drops vanilla essence
2tbsp/30ml brandy
3-4tbsp/45ml-60ml milk
5fl.ozs/150ml double cream
About 24 ratafia biscuits or sponge fingers

Prepare the redcurrants, rinse in cold water and drain thoroughly, reserving a few for decoration. Beat together the cream cheese, sugar and vanilla essence in a bowl and then add the brandy a tablespoonful at a time and continue to beat. Whisk the cream and fold into the cheese mixture. Set aside to chill and mixture will thicken. Put the mixture into individual serving bowls, arrange the biscuits around the sides and fill the centres with the redcurrants. Cover with the remaining cheese mixture and decorate with reserved redcurrants. Place in a refrigerator until ready to serve.

RED CURRANT CREAM (serves 4)

1lb/500g redcurrants
½ pint/300ml fresh double cream
5ozs/125g castor sugar

Press the fruit through a sieve and mix the purée with the sugar. Whisk the cream and stir in the sweetened purée. Put in a serving dish and keep refrigerated until ready to serve.

FRUIT FOOL (serves 4)

½ ounce/12g powdered gelatine
5tbsp/75ml water
1lb/500g rhubarb
4tbsp/60ml redcurrant jelly
7oz/200g fromage frais
Red food colouring (if desired)
4tbsp/60ml natural yoghurt

Put the gelatine and water in a small bowl and leave to soak. Prepare the rhubarb, cut into chunks and put in a saucepan, adding the redcurrant jelly. Bring to the boil and simmer for 15 minutes or until soft, stirring occasionally. Remove from heat and add the dissolved gelatine. Mix well and leave to cool slightly. Then put the cooked rhubarb into a food processor, blend to make a purée and put in a bowl to cool. When mixture is cold, stir in the fromage frais and add the food colouring if you wish. Put in a serving dish or individual dishes and place in refrigerator for about 3 hours before serving. Serve with the yoghurt.

CHANTILLY GOOSEBERRIES (serves 4)

1lb/500g gooseberries
7ozs/200g castor sugar
¼ pint/150ml double cream

Prepare the gooseberries and put in a pan with a little water. Cook fruit gently until very soft and leave to stand for about half an hour. Mash the fruit, add the sugar and leave to get cold. Put in serving dishes and cover with the whipped cream.

GOOSEBERRY FOOL (serves 4)

1lb/500g gooseberries
Sugar to taste
½ pint/300ml whipped double cream

Set oven at 330F/160C/Gas Mark 3

Put the gooseberries in a covered ovenproof dish with sugar to taste and heat in a warm oven until the juice runs. Press the fruit through a sieve and allow to cool. When cold, mix thoroughly with the whipped cream and put into individual serving dishes.

GOOSEBERRY CREAM (serves 6-8)

2lbs/900g gooseberries
½ pint/300ml water
Sugar to taste
1oz/25g butter
2 eggs
1 dsp/10ml Orange flower water
Green food colouring (if desired)

Put the gooseberries in a saucepan with the water and cook until soft enough to press through a sieve. Reheat the purée, sweeten to taste and add the butter, mixing well. Beat the eggs and add them to the purée, stirring continuously. Do not allow mixture to boil. When it has thickened, remove from heat and leave to cool. Add the orange flower water and a little green food colouring if desired. Stir well and pour into serving glasses. Delicious served with cream and sponge fingers.

SUMMER SPECIAL (serves 4-6)

8ozs/250g strawberries
Castor sugar to taste
12ozs/350g raspberries
1/4 pint/150ml double cream

To make the strawberry purée, process the strawberries in a food processor and add sugar to taste (this should produce about 1/4 pint/150ml of purée). Arrange the raspberries in serving dishes. Whip the cream and add the strawberry purée and continue to whip until the mixture holds it shape. Spoon over the raspberries and decorate as desired.

SCOTTISH DELIGHT (serves 4)

3-4ozs/75-100g toasted oatmeal
1/2 pint/300ml double cream
1 tbsp/15ml rum
4-6ozs/125-175g raspberries or blackberries (reserve a few for decoration)

Toast the oatmeal in a pan until light brown. Lightly whip the cream and add the rum, fold in the oatmeal and then the fruit. Put into individual serving glasses and decorate with reserved fruit.

TIPSY BERRIES (serves 4)

1lb/500g strawberries
Castor sugar (for dusting)
Juice of ½ orange
1-2tbsp/15-30ml Kirsch
8ozs/250g raspberries
2ozs/125g icing sugar
½ pint/300ml double cream

Prepare the strawberries and place in a bowl. Dust with the castor sugar and sprinkle over the orange juice and kirsch. Cover and leave in a cool place. Rub the raspberries through a sieve to make a purée and gradually add the icing sugar, mixing all the time. Lightly whip the cream and fold into the raspberry purée. Spoon over the strawberries and serve.

RASPBERRIES WITH AVOCADO CREAM (serves 4)

4ozs/125g avocado
4ozs/125g curd cheese
1oz/25g castor sugar
Juice of 1 lemon
6tbsp/90ml single cream
1lb/500g raspberries

Mash the avocado and curd cheese in a bowl until smooth. Mix the sugar, lemon juice and cream into the avocado and cheese mix, stirring thoroughly. Arrange the raspberries in serving dishes and top with the cream mixture. Leave in a cool place until ready to serve.

RASPBERRY CREAM SUNDAE (*serves 4*)

2 eggs
1oz/25g cornflour
½ pint/300ml skimmed milk
Sugar to taste
15oz/450g raspberries

Blend the cornflour with 1 egg yolk and 1 whole egg and add a little milk to make a smooth paste. Put the remaining milk in a saucepan, heat and when just below boiling gradually pour in the cornflour paste, stirring continuously. Return pan to the heat and continue stirring while mixture cooks and thickens. Remove from heat and add sugar to taste. Pour into a bowl and leave to cool, covering with cling film. Just before serving, whisk the remaining egg white until stiff and fold carefully into the cold sauce. Fold in the raspberries and spoon into serving dishes.

CHANTILLY RASPBERRIES

1lb/500g raspberries
2tbsp/30ml water
5ozs/140g castor sugar
½ pint/300ml fresh cream

Sort the fruit, extracting the firmer raspberries, and put the remainder through a sieve. Put the firm fruit in serving glasses. Cook the puréed raspberries with the water and sugar for a few minutes and leave to cool. When cold spoon over the whole fruit and pour the lightly whipped cream on top. Serve immediately.

RASPBERRY CREAM (serves 4)

12ozs/375g raspberries
4ozs/125g castor sugar
½ pint/300ml double cream
A few whole raspberries for decoration

Rinse the raspberries in cold water, place them in a saucepan with the sugar and cook gently until the fruit is soft. Put the fruit through a sieve to make a purée and leave to get cold. Whisk the cream until thick and stir three-quarters of it into the raspberry purée. Spoon into individual serving bowls and chill in a refrigerator. Decorate with the remaining cream and reserved raspberries.

STRAWBERRIES ROMANOFF (serves 6-8)

2lbs/950g strawberries (washed and hulled)
1pt/600ml vanilla ice cream
½ pint/300ml whipped double cream
Juice of 1 lemon
2tbsp/30ml rum or Cointreau
Sugar to taste

Beat the ice cream with a fork to soften and fold in the whipped cream. Gently stir in the lemon juice and rum or Cointreau. Check for taste and add sugar if desired. Carefully fold in the strawberries and serve immediately.

STRAWBERRIES IN SHERRY CREAM (serves 6-8)

5 egg yolks
8ozs/250g castor sugar
8fl.ozs/275ml sherry
½ pint/300ml whipped double cream
3lbs/1.5kgs strawberries (washed and hulled)

Put the egg yolks in a double boiler or in a bowl stood in a pan of gently bubbling water. Beat yolks with a whisk until thick and lemon coloured. Add the sugar and sherry and continue to stir until mixture thickens. Allow to cool. When ready to serve, fold in the cream and prepared fruit and spoon into a glass serving dish.

BRANDIED STRAWBERRIES (serves 4)

1lb/500g strawberries
6-8 sugar lumps
1 large orange
4tbsp/60ml brandy

Prepare the strawberries and place in a serving bowl. Rub the sugar lumps over the orange rind until they have absorbed the oil and squeeze the juice from the orange. Break down the sugar lumps, add the orange juice and brandy and mix well. Pour brandy and orange mixture over the strawberries and leave to chill for about 2-3 hours before serving.

CORDON BLEU STRAWBERRIES (serves 4)

1lb/500g strawberries
1 orange
2ozs/125g castor sugar
¼ pint/150ml double cream

Prepare the strawberries and place in a serving bowl. Grate the rind finely from the orange and squeeze the juice from one half of the fruit. Put the juice, sugar and rind in a small basin and, using a wooden spoon, stir until the sugar is dissolved. Lightly whip the cream, fold in the syrup mix and then spoon over the strawberries. Allow to chill for at least half an hour before serving.

STRAWBERRY CREAM (serves 3-4)

8ozs/250g strawberries
½ pint/300ml cream
½ ounce/13g gelatine
3ozs/75g castor sugar
Juice of ½ lemon
4fl.ozs/150ml milk

Prepare the strawberries and press through a sieve. Add the sugar and lemon juice to the purée and mix well. Soak the gelatine in a little water, add it to the milk and strain on to the puréed strawberries. Whip the cream and mix into the strawberry mixture. Pour the mixture into a wetted mould and place in a refrigerator to set. When ready to serve turn out carefully on to a serving dish and decorate as desired.

STRAWBERRIES WITH SHORTBREAD (serves 4-6)

3ozs/90g plain flour
1½ozs/40g margarine
½ teaspoon lemon juice
Vanilla essence
2ozs/50g castor sugar
1½lbs/750g strawberries
6fl.ozs/225ml double cream
2fl.ozs/75ml natural yoghurt

Set oven at 350F/180C/Gas Mark 4.
To make the shortbread, sieve the flour into a bowl, add the softened margarine, lemon juice, vanilla essence and half the sugar. Blend all the ingredients together. Put the mixture onto a floured board, knead lightly and then roll out to make a rectangle about 7"x5" (175x125cm). Cut the mixture into six rectangles and mark across each one to make two triangular biscuits in each rectangle. Transfer carefully to a lined baking sheet and bake for about 12-15 minutes. When golden brown remove from oven and place on a wire rack to cool.

Divide the strawberries into individual serving glasses and sprinkle over the remaining sugar. Whip the cream until thick, add the yoghurt gradually and whisk until firm. Spoon the mixture on top of the strawberries and put shortbread triangles at the side of each glass.

STRAWBERRIES IN WHIPPED CREAM (serves 6-8)

2lbs/900g strawberries
½ pint/300ml double cream
Sugar to taste
Flavouring of your choice - vanilla, brandy, cointreau, sherry ....

Prepare the strawberries, cut in half and sprinkle with sugar. Whip the cream until firm, sweeten if desired and add flavouring of your choice. Fold in the halved strawberries and serve in individual dishes or one glass serving bowl. Put in a cool place for about an hour before serving.

Ices and Frozen Desserts

BLACKBERRY ICE CREAM (serves 8)

1lb/500g blackberries
2ozs/50g castor sugar
4fl.ozs/120ml water
2ozs/50g granulated sugar
3 egg yolks
12fl.ozs/450ml single cream
2ozs/50g icing sugar
2tbsp/30ml rose water

Put the blackberries in a saucepan with the sugar and cook gently until tender. Press through a sieve and allow purée to cool. Put the water and granulated sugar in a pan and heat gradually until the sugar is dissolved. Bring to the boil and continue to boil steadily until it forms a syrup. To test the syrup, allow a little to cool and using thumb and forefinger draw it up to form a thread. Remove syrup from heat and allow to cool. Break the egg yolks into a bowl, add the syrup and whisk briskly until the mixture is thick and frothy. Mix the cream and blackberry purée together and fold into the mousse mixture.

Put mixture into a freezerproof container, cover, seal and freeze. Transfer ice cream to the refrigerator for about an hour before serving and scoop into individual glasses. Serve with wafer biscuits.

BLACKBERRY SORBET (serves 4)

1pt/600ml blackberry juice
3ozs/75g sugar
½ ounce/13g powdered gelatine
1tbsp/15ml water
1 egg white

To make blackberry juice put the berries in a covered casserole dish and put in a slow oven until the juice runs freely. Pour cooked blackberries into a jelly bag and allow it to drip overnight into a bowl.

Put the sugar and juice into a saucepan but do not allow to boil too much. Dissolve the gelatine in the water and add to the fruit liquid. Stir well until all is dissolved and then allow to cool. When almost on the point of setting, whisk in a liquidiser or food processor. Beat the egg white and add to the blackberry mixture. Pour into a freezer mould and put in freezer.

BLUEBERRY ICE CREAM (serve 4-6)

2lbs/950g blueberries
8ozs/250g sugar
1pt/600ml thin cream

Put the prepared blueberries in a saucepan and cook until soft. Add the sugar, mash the berries and put through a sieve. Stir in the cream and pour into a freezer mould.

CURRANT SORBET (serves 4)

1lb/500g black, red or mixed currants
8ozs/250g granulated sugar
½ pint/300ml cold water

Mash the currants and then put through a sieve to remove the skins and seeds. Put the sugar and water in a pan, heat gently until the sugar is dissolved and then bring to the boil. Boil rapidly for 5 minutes and then leave to cool. When syrup is quite cold, add to the currant purée and whisk. Pour into a plastic dish and put in the freezer until it is half frozen. Remove and whisk again and then return it to the freezer to set.

GOOSEBERRY SORBET (serves 4)

1lb/500g gooseberries
4ozs/125g sugar
5fl.ozs/150ml water
Juice and grated zest of 1 lemon
2 egg whites

Prepare the gooseberries, wash them under cold water and reserve a few for decoration. Put the remaining gooseberries in a saucepan with the sugar, water, lemon juice and zest. Stew gently for 20 minutes. Put the gooseberries in a food processor, reduce them to a purée and pour into an ice tray. When the mixture is partially set, whisk the egg whites until very stiff and fold into the purée. Return to the ice tray and freeze until solid. Serve in individual chilled glasses and decorate with the reserved gooseberries.

GOOSEBERRY ICE CREAM (serve 6-8)

12ozs/375g gooseberries
2fl.oz/60ml water
7oz/220g sugar
2 egg yolks
8fl.ozs/250ml milk
8fl.ozs/250ml cream
Vanilla essence to taste

Put the prepared gooseberries in a saucepan with the water and a quarter of the sugar and heat gradually, dissolving the sugar. Bring to the boil, cover and allow to simmer very gently until the fruit is soft. Allow to cool. Put the cooked fruit in a food processor or blender to make a purée and then strain to remove seeds and skins.

Whisk the remaining sugar and egg yolks in a metal bowl until thick and smooth. In a small pan bring the milk to almost boiling point and add to the sugar and egg yolks. Place the bowl in a pan of simmering water and stir continuously until the mixture thickens. Remove from heat and stir in the fruit purée, cream and vanilla essence. Pour mixture into an ice cream container and freeze.

NB. Blackcurrants may be used instead of gooseberries.

RASPBERRY ICE

4lbs/2kgs raspberries
1lb/500g sugar
Few grains salt
1pint/600ml water
Lemon juice to taste

Prepare the raspberries, put in a bowl and cover with the sugar. Allow to stand for two hours and then mash and press through a sieve. To the purée add the salt, water and lemon juice and mix well. Pour into a freezer container and freeze.

NB. Strawberries will do just as well for this ice.

RICH FRUIT ICE CREAM

3 egg yolks
2ozs/50g icing sugar
1tbsp/15ml lemon juice
1/4 pint/150ml whipped cream
8ozs/250g strawberries or raspberries

Put the egg yolks and sugar in a bowl stood in simmering water and beat until thick and creamy. Purée the fruit in a liquidiser or food processor and then sieve to remove pips. Mix the lemon juice into the purée and lightly fold in the egg and sugar mixture and the cream. Pour into a container and freeze.

FRUIT WATER ICE

8ozs/250g granulated sugar
½ pint/300ml water
Juice of 1 lemon
Juice of 1 orange
1lb/500g raspberries, strawberries or other soft fruit

To make the syrup, dissolve the sugar in the water in a pan, bring to the boil and simmer for about five minutes. Allow to cool and add the lemon and orange juice. Put the fruit in a liquidiser or food processor and then through a sieve to remove the pips. Mix the fruit purée and syrup together and pour into a container and freeze.

RASPBERRY BAVAROISE (serves 4)

1lb/500g raspberries
½ pint/300ml fresh cream
1pint/600ml milk
4 egg yolks
5ozs/150g sugar
Few drops of vanilla essence

Put the milk, sugar and egg yolks in a pan and heat gently, stirring continuously until the mixture becomes creamy. Add a few drops of vanilla essence and leave to cool. Pass the raspberries through a sieve and then add the purée to the milk, sugar and egg yolks. Mix well and fold in the beaten cream. Pour into a container and freeze.

RASPBERRY ICE CREAM

2lbs/500g raspberries
8ozs/250g sugar
1pt/600ml thin cream
1/4 teaspoon salt

Put the raspberries in a bowl, sprinkle over the sugar and leave to stand for at least half an hour. Then press the raspberries through a sieve to remove the pips. Add the cream to the purée and mix thoroughly and add the salt and extra sugar if needed. Turn into a container and freeze.

NB. Strawberries can also be used for this recipe.

RASPBERRY SORBET (serves 4-6)

10ozs/310g raspberries
8fl.oz/250ml sugar syrup
1 egg white (whisked)

Sugar syrup can be made by allowing 1lb/500g sugar to every 16fl.oz/450ml water. Put the water and sugar in a saucepan, bring to the boil and reduce heat. Allow to simmer for 10 minutes and then leave to cool. Once cooled the syrup may be kept in a covered container in a refrigerator for about 2-3 weeks.

Put the raspberries and sugar syrup in a food processor and blend to make a purée. Pour into an ice tray, cover, put in the freezer and leave until it is "slushy". Return the semi frozen purée to the food processor and blend with the egg white. Return mixture to the ice tray, cover and freeze until firm.

RASPBERRY PARFAIT (serves 4)

1lb/500g raspberries
2 egg whites
4oz/125g castor sugar
10fl.oz/300ml double cream (lightly whipped)
1 tbsp/15ml Cointreau
Wafer biscuits to serve

Press the raspberries through a sieve, put the purée in a freezerproof container, cover and freeze for 1-2 hours until partially frozen. Whisk the egg whites until stiff and gradually add the sugar, continuing to whisk until mixture is very stiff, and then carefully fold in the cream. Remove the half-frozen purée from the freezer and beat with a fork. Add the purée and Cointreau to the cream and egg white mixture and fold in carefully. Spoon mixture into serving glasses and serve immediately garnished with wafer biscuits.

RASPBERRY WATER ICE

8ozs/250g granulated sugar
½ pint/300ml cold water
1lb/500g raspberries
3tbsp/45ml water
2 large egg whites (whisked)
½ ounce/15g castor sugar

Make a syrup by putting the ½ pint/300ml water and granulated sugar in a saucepan, heat gradually to dissolve the sugar, bring to the boil and then allow to simmer for about 5 minutes or until syrupy. Remove from heat and leave to cool. Prepare the raspberries and reserve a few good ones for decoration. Place the remainder in a saucepan with the 3 tablespoons/45ml water and heat gently until the fruit begins to soften and the juice runs. Press fruit through a sieve into a bowl and then whisk in the syrup. Put the mixture in a freezerproof container, cover and freeze for about 2 hours or until partially frozen. Remove semi-frozen mixture from the freezer and tip into a bowl. Whisk in the egg whites and return to the covered freezer container. Freeze for 3-4 hours or until solid. When ready to serve, garnish with the reserved raspberries and sprinkle over the castor sugar.

STRAWBERRY SORBET (serves 6-8)

1lb.4ozs/625g strawberries
16fl.ozs/500ml sugar syrup (as for the Raspberry Sorbet see page 58)
Juice of ½ an orange
Juice of ½ a lemon

Hull the strawberries and reserve a few firm ones for decoration. Place remaining strawberries in a food processor with half the sugar syrup to make a smooth purée. Stir in the remaining syrup with the orange and lemon juice. Pour into a freezerproof container, cover and freeze until partially frozen. Return mixture to the food processor and process again until light and smooth. Return mixture to the ice tray and re-freeze until firm. Garnish with reserved strawberries when ready to serve.

STRAWBERRY ICE CREAM (serves 6-8)

1lb/500g strawberries
4ozs/125g sugar
12fl.ozs/350ml whipping cream (lightly whipped)

Prepare the strawberries and mash down. Process mashed strawberries with the sugar in a food processor until smooth. Fold the purée into the cream and pour mixture into a freezerproof container, cover and freeze until firm, allowing 3-6 hours. Whilst freezing, remove from freezer two or three times and beat with a fork.

STRAWBERRY BAVAROISE (serves 4-6)

1lb/500g strawberries
½ pint/300ml double cream
1pt/600ml milk
5ozs/150g sugar
4 egg yolks
Few drops vanilla essence

Put the milk, sugar and vanilla essence in a saucepan and bring to the boil. Put the egg yolks in a separate pan and pour the heated milk over them. Heat the mixture slowly, stirring constantly until it thickens, pass it through a sieve and leave to cool. Wash and hull the strawberries and purée in a food processor and mix in the well beaten cream. Add to the vanilla mixture and stir well. Pour into a mould, cover and place in a freezer until ready to serve.

STRAWBERRY PARFAIT (serves 6-8)

2lbs/1kg strawberries
8ozs/250g sugar
½ pint/300ml water
3 egg whites (whisked until very stiff)
1pint/600ml double cream

Wash, hull and mash the strawberries and sprinkle over half the sugar. Leave for a few hours and then strain through a sieve. Place in a freezer tray, cover and allow to partially set. Make the syrup with the remaining sugar and water, bring to the boil in a pan and boil for about 5 minutes. Pour the syrup slowly over the firmly whisked egg whites and beat the mixture until cool. Fold the cream into the mixture and then the partially frozen strawberry purée. Pour the mixture into a covered freezer container and freeze until firm.

INDIVIDUAL STRAWBERRY ALASKAS (serves 4)

8ozs/250g strawberries
1 egg white
Pinch of cream of tartar
2ozs/50g castor sugar
4oz/125g ice cream (not soft scoop variety)

Hull the strawberries, slice and set aside. Whisk the egg white with the cream of tartar until stiff, add half the sugar, whisk again, add remaining sugar and whisk until mixture is very stiff. Divide the ice cream into four ramekin dishes and scatter the sliced strawberries over the ice cream. Spoon the whisked egg white on top and draw up into peaks. Place dishes under a preheated grill for 1-2 minutes until golden brown and serve immediately.

STRAWBERRY BOMBE (serves 8-10)

8ozs/250g sieved strawberries
8fl.ozs/225ml double cream
1tbsp/15ml kirsch
2tsp/10ml vanilla essence
6ozs/175g icing sugar
2pts/1.2l strawberry ice (see recipe for fruit water ice page 57)
Whipped cream
A few whole strawberries

Stir the sieved strawberries into the whipped double cream and add the kirsch, vanilla essence and icing sugar. Mix well. Line a 4pt/2.5l mould with the strawberry ice and fill with the prepared strawberry cream. Cover and freeze. When ready to serve, garnish with the whipped cream and whole strawberries.

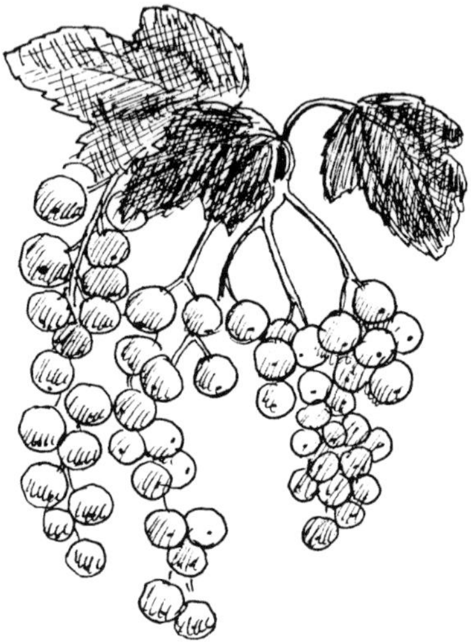

Pies, Flans & Cheesecakes

BLACKBERRY PIE

BLUEBERRY PIE

BLACKBERRY PIE (serves 6)

8ozs/250g plain flour
Pinch salt
6ozs/175g margarine/butter/shortening (whichever is your preference) or a mixture of two
Ice cold water
1lb/500g blackberries
Sugar to taste

Cook the blackberries in a little water and add sugar to taste. Set aside to cool.
Sift the flour and salt into a mixing bowl and add the fat, cut into small pieces. Rub the fat into the flour using hands or a fork and then gradually add ice cold water until a firm mixture is formed (handle the pastry as little as possible). Wrap in cling film and chill for about half an hour.

Set oven at 350F/180C/Gas Mark 4.

Roll out pastry on a floured board and using two-thirds, line a greased pie dish. Pour in the cooked blackberries and moisten the edge of the pie. Place the remaining pastry over the top, pinch edges to seal, prick pastry to release steam whilst cooking and sprinkle a little sugar on top. Cook for 40-50 minutes when it should be golden brown. Serve hot or cold with cream or custard.

BLUEBERRY PIE (serves 6)

Shortcrust pastry as for the Blackberry Pie
1lb/500g blueberries
2ozs/50g flour
6ozs/175g sugar
Pinch salt
A little lemon juice
A knob of butter

Set oven at 350F/180C/Gas Mark 4

Discard the stems and leaves of the fruit, wash well and put in a bowl. Add the flour, sugar and pinch of salt and mix well. Make the pastry as for the Blackberry Pie and fill pie dish with the blueberries. Sprinkle over with the lemon juice and knob of butter before putting on the top crust and pricking pastry top. Cook for 40-50 minutes when it should be golden brown. Best served hot with cream or custard.

LEMON AND BLACKCURRANT CHEESECAKE (serves 6-8)

3ozs/75g margarine
6ozs/175g castor sugar
6ozs/175g crushed digestive biscuits
8ozs/250g low-fat soft cheese
Grated rind and juice of 1 lemon
3 eggs (separated)
1oz/25g plain flour
4ozs/125g blackcurrants

Melt the margarine in a saucepan and mix in 2ozs/50g of the sugar and crushed biscuits. Press the mixture over the base of a greased loose-bottomed 8"/20cm round cake tin. Put in a refrigerator to chill.

Set oven at 350F/180C/Gas Mark 4.

Put the cheese, lemon rind and juice, egg yolks and 2ozs/50g of the sugar in a bowl and beat well. Whisk the egg whites until firm and whisk in the remaining sugar. Fold egg white mixture into the cheese mixture and stir in the blackcurrants. Spread over the biscuit base. Bake in the oven for about 1¼ hours or until well risen and fairly firm. Reduce heat to 325F/170C/Gas Mark 3 and cook for a further 30 minutes or until really firm. Cover lightly with foil whilst cooking to prevent top browning too much. Remove from the oven and leave to stand for a few minutes. Using a palette knife ease sides of the cheesecake away from the tin and carefully push cake out on its base. Slide it off the base and leave to cool. Dust with icing sugar when ready to serve.

LUXURY BLACKCURRANT CHEESECAKE (serves 6)

4ozs/125g butter
8ozs/250g ginger biscuits (crushed)
1lb/500g soft cheese
2ozs/50g castor sugar
6tbsp/90ml single cream
1lb4ozs/575g blackcurrants
½ ounce/13g gelatine
2tbsp/30ml hot water
½ pint/300ml double cream
1 egg white (stiffly whisked)

Lightly grease a 9"/23cm loose-bottomed cake tin with a little of the butter and melt the remainder in a small saucepan. Add the crushed ginger biscuits and mix well. Press mixture firmly into the base of the tin and chill until set.

Prepare the blackcurrants. Put the soft cheese and sugar in a bowl and beat until smooth and creamy. Stir in the single cream and the blackcurrants. Dissolve the gelatine in the hot water and stir into the blackcurrant mixture. Spoon over the biscuit base and return the cheesecake to the refrigerator to chill for at least an hour. Whip the double cream and swirl it over the cheesecake. Decorate with a few reserved blackcurrants.

BLACKCURRANT FLAN (serves 4-6)

For the base -
6ozs/175g plain flour
2tsp ground cinnamon
4ozs/125g butter
1oz/25g castor sugar
1 egg yolk
2tsp/10ml water

For the filling -
1lb/500g blackcurrants (destalked and washed)
4ozs/25g demerara sugar

Sift the flour and cinnamon into a bowl and rub in the butter until the mixture resembles breadcrumbs. Stir in the castor sugar, add the egg yolk and water and mix to make a firm dough. Knead it very lightly, roll it out on a floured board and then line a 7"/18cm flan ring. Chill the flan for about 15 minutes with the pastry trimmings.

Cook the blackcurrants and demerara sugar covered in a pan for about 10 minutes, remove cover and turn up the heat. Continue to cook until the fruit mixture is thick and syrupy but stir frequently to prevent it sticking to the pan. Remove from heat to cool.

Set oven at 400F/200C/Gas Mark 6.

Put the cooled fruit mixture in the flan case and roll out and cut the pastry trimmings into strips to make a lattice pattern on top of the fruit. Brush with water and sprinkle over with castor sugar. Bake for 25 to 30 minutes until golden brown. Can be served hot or cold with whipped cream.

GOOSEBERRY PIE

1lb/500g gooseberries (topped and tailed)
5ozs/150g sugar
2tbsp/30ml beer or light ale
6ozs/175g plain flour
4ozs/125g lard/margarine/butter
Cold water

Grease a pie dish and fill with the gooseberries. Sprinkle over the sugar and beer or light ale. Make the short crust pastry with the flour, fat and cold water and cover the pie dish. Seal the edges by wetting the pie dish and pinching the edges. Prick the pastry to release the steam from the fruit.
Set oven at 400F/200C/Gas Mark 6.
Bake pie for about 30 minutes and serve hot or cold.

NB. Try a few elderberries added to the gooseberries for a slight difference.

GOOSEBERRY TART

8ozs/250g self-raising flour
5ozs/150g butter
4ozs/125g castor sugar
Pinch of salt
1 egg yolk
8fl.ozs/230ml single cream
8ozs/250g gooseberries (topped and tailed)

Set oven at 350F/180C/Gas Mark 4.

Make a paste with the flour, butter, castor sugar, salt, egg yolk and cream and roll out about quarter inch/5mm thick. Grease a tart tin and line with the paste. Place the gooseberries in the lined tin and sprinkle over with a little sugar. Brush the edges of the tart with a little egg yolk and bake for about 45 minutes until golden brown. Serve hot or cold.

RASPBERRY AND ALMOND TART

1lb/500g raspberries
Sugar to taste
8ozs/250g plain flour
Pinch salt
1 tsp cinnamon
2½ozs/130g ground almonds
4ozs/125g butter
4ozs/125g castor sugar
1 whole egg
1 egg yolk
Grated rind of half a lemon
Redcurrant jelly

Put the raspberries and sugar in a pan, bring to the boil and cook rapidly for 4-5 minutes to thicken the mixture. Pour out onto a dish to cool. Sieve the flour, salt and cinnamon onto a board in a circle and sprinkle with the ground almonds. In the centre, place the butter, sugar, whole egg and egg yolk and lemon rind and gradually work in the ingredients to form a dough. Wrap in cling film and leave in a cool place for about an hour.

Set oven at 375F/190C/Gas Mark 5.

Roll out the chilled dough about quarter inch/5mm thick and line a 7"/18cm flan ring. Trim the edges and fill with the cold raspberry mixture. Roll out the trimmings, cut into strips and make a lattice across the top. Bake for 25-30 minutes. Remove from the oven and allow to cool before removing carefully from the flan ring. Brush over the top with the melted redcurrant jelly.

SCOTTISH CHEESECAKE (serves 6-8)

4ozs/125g butter
1/4 pint/150ml whisky
8ozs/250g digestive biscuits (crushed)
8ozs/250g cream cheese
2ozs/50g castor sugar
1/2 pint/300ml double cream
8ozs/250g raspberries
2tbsp/30ml honey
3tsp/15ml arrowroot
1tsp castor sugar
1/4 pint/150ml whipping cream

Melt the butter in a saucepan, add 1 tablespoon/15ml whisky and stir in the crushed biscuits. Press mixture firmly into a greased loose-bottomed 8"/20cm cake tin and put in refrigerator to chill for about 30 minutes. Make the filling by beating the cream cheese and 2ozs/50g castor sugar together until smooth. Whip the double cream and 1 tablespoon/15ml whisky together until stiff and fold into the cream cheese mixture. Spoon over the biscuit base and leave to chill.

Mix the honey and 6 tablespoons/90ml whisky. Put the raspberries in a bowl and pour over the honey and whisky mixture. Leave for 30 minutes and then strain the raspberries which should leave 4fl.ozs/125ml of liquid (top up with whisky if not quite enough). Blend the arrowroot with 2 tablespoons/30ml of the juice and put the remaining juice in a saucepan with the teaspoon of castor sugar. Bring to almost boiling point and add the arrowroot paste, reduce the heat and continue stirring until the glaze is thick. Stir the strained raspberries into the glaze and then set aside to cool. Spoon the raspberry glaze over the cheesecake and decorate with the cream which has been whipped up with the remaining whisky. Sprinkle with a little malt whisky before serving if desired.

SCOTTISH RASPBERRY TART (serves 4-6)

3½ozs/115g butter
7ozs/200g digestive biscuits (crushed)
1oz/25g toasted sesame seeds
3tbsp/45ml whisky
1-2tbsp/15-30ml lemon juice
2tbsp/30ml clear honey
¼ pint/150ml double cream
Fresh raspberries

Melt the butter in a saucepan and stir in the crushed biscuits and sesame seeds. Press mixture into the base and up the side of a lightly creased 8"/20cm flan dish. Put in a refrigerator to cool while make the filling. Put the whisky, lemon juice and honey into a bowl and whisk until well blended. Add the cream and continue whisking until fairly firm. Spoon onto the chilled base and return to the refrigerator for 1-2 hours to set. Top with the fresh raspberries before serving.

FRESH RASPBERRY TART

8ozs/250g self-raising flour
5ozs/150g butter
4ozs/125g castor sugar
Pinch of salt
1 egg yolk
8fl.ozs/250ml cream
8ozs/250g raspberries
A little extra sugar
Set oven at 350F/180C/Gas Mark 4

Make the paste as for the Gooseberry tart (page 68) using the flour, butter, castor sugar, salt, egg yolk and cream and line a tart tin with the paste. Prepare the raspberries, place on the paste and sprinkle over a little sugar. Brush the edges with egg yolk. Bake for about 45 minutes until golden brown at the edges. Serve hot or cold.

RASPBERRY ANGEL PIE

4 egg whites
Pinch salt
1/4 teaspoon cream of tartar
8ozs/250g granulated sugar
1/2 teaspoon vanilla essence
8fl.ozs/250ml whipped cream
Firm fresh raspberries
A little sugar

Whisk the egg whites with the salt and cream of tartar until very stiff and gradually beat in the sugar and vanilla essence. Spread mixture on baking paper, making the edge higher to form a rim. Bake in the slow oven until dry and firm to the touch but not brown. Leave to cool.

Whip the cream and prepare the raspberries. Using half the cream, spread it in the meringue shell, cover with the raspberries and sprinkle over with castor sugar. Cover with the remaining cream and decorate with a few reserved raspberries. Serve immediately.

NB.Strawberries can also be used for this recipe but should be sliced or halved.

RASPBERRY AND ALMOND FLAN (serves 6-8)

8ozs/250g raspberries

For the pastry -
3ozs/75g butter
1oz/25g vegetable shortening
6ozs/150g plain flour
1½ozs/35g ground almonds
1½ozs/35g castor sugar
Few drops vanilla essence
1 large egg yolk
1-2tbsp/15-30ml cold water

For the meringue -
3 small egg whites
6ozs/150g castor sugar
6ozs/150g ground almonds

To decorate -
½ pint/300ml double cream
Castor sugar to taste
Few drops vanilla essence
Shredded almonds (browned)

To make the pastry, rub the fats into the flour and mix in the ground almonds and sugar. Mix the egg yolk and vanilla essence with the water and add to the dry ingredients. Knead lightly until it forms a firm paste, wrap in cling film and leave to chill for about 15 minutes.

Set the oven at 350F/180C/Gas Mark 4.

Roll out the pastry and line a flan ring, pricking the bottom lightly. Cover with the raspberries. To make the almond meringue, whip the egg whites until firm and continuing to whisk, add the sugar a little at a time. Fold in the ground almonds and spread the mixture over the raspberries. Bake for about 30 minutes. Leave to cool in the tin and then remove carefully. When ready to serve, whip the cream, slightly sweetened and flavoured with the essence and cover the flan. Decorate with the browned almonds.

STRAWBERRY MILK PUDDING

1lb/500g paste (as for the Gooseberry Tart on page 68)
8ozs/250g strawberries
2ozs/50g castor sugar
1oz/25g flour
½ pint/300ml milk
1 egg
1oz/25g butter
Few drops of vanilla essence or 2tbsp/30ml rum

Cook the tart with the strawberries as for the Gooseberry tart. To prepare the topping, cream the sugar and egg together in a saucepan, then add the flour and slowly pour over the boiling milk and the vanilla essence if using, stirring constantly, while mixture thickens. Remove from the heat and add the butter cut into small pieces and the rum if not using vanilla essence. Pour the creamed mixture over the strawberry tart and put in a warm oven for few minutes to lightly brown. Serve immediately.

FRENCH GLACÉ TART (serves 6-8)

13ozs/370g packet of puff pastry
1 egg yolk mixed with 1tsp/5ml of water
4tbsp/60ml apricot jam
2tbsp/30ml water
1tsp/5ml lemon juice
4ozs/125g black seedless grapes
4ozs/125g white seedless grapes
4ozs/125g strawberries

Roll out the pastry to make a rectangle about 12"x8" (30x20cm), sprinkle the pastry with flour and fold in half lengthways. Cut out a rectangle from the folded edge leaving a 1.5"/3.5cm wide band on the three remaining sides. Open out the cut out rectangle and roll out until it is the same size as the original (12"x8") and place on a dampened baking sheet. Brush the edges lightly with water and place the band of pastry over the top, making a border. Score the edges lightly with a knife to make a pattern and brush over with the egg and water mixture to glaze. Leave pastry to rest for about 15 minutes.

Set oven at 425F/220C/Gas Mark 7 and bake pastry case for 20-25 minutes until golden brown. Set aside to cool.

Heat the jam with the water and lemon juice, pass through a sieve and re-heat to make a clear glaze. Brush the base of the pastry case with the glaze and arrange the fruit to your liking in the base. Brush generously with the glaze and serve tart cold.

STRAWBERRY AND ALMOND TARTS

Shortcrust pastry as for the Blackberry Pie on page 64
Strawberry jam
2ozs/50g butter
6ozs/175g castor sugar
Pinch salt
2 eggs (well beaten)
1oz/25g flour
1tsp/5ml almond essence

Set oven at 425F/220C/Gas Mark 7.

Cut pastry to line small deep tart tins and put a teaspoon of strawberry jam in the bottom of each one. Cream the butter and sugar together and stir in the salt, eggs, flour and almond essence, mixing well. Fill the tarts about two-thirds full. Bake for about 13-15 minutes until golden brown. If serving as a dessert, garnish with whipped cream and chopped toasted almonds.

INDIVIDUAL STRAWBERRIES WITH SHORTBREAD (serves 4)

For the shortbread -
6ozs/175g plain flour
4ozs/125g butter
2ozs/50g castor sugar

For the sauce -
1/4 pint/150ml double cream
3-4tbsp/45-60ml orange juice
3-4tbsp/45-60ml orange flavoured liqueur

4 good strawberries with stalks on
2ozs/50g castor sugar
4tbsp/60ml water

Set oven at 300F/150C/Gas Mark 2.

To make the shortbread, sieve the flour into a bowl and rub in the butter until the mixture forms a "breadcrumb" texture. Add the sugar and knead in well until the dough is soft and pliable. Add a little more flour if the dough is a little sticky. Divide the mixture in half and roll out each into two thin rounds. Make 6 triangles on each round, pricking with a fork and bake for about 35-45 minutes or until golden brown and crisp.

Beat the cream until thick and add the orange juice and liqueur. Dissolve the sugar in the water, bring to the boil and continue cooking until the mixture becomes syrupy.

Using individual serving glasses pour in a layer of the orange cream. Arrange three triangles of shortbread on the top. Dip each strawberry in the syrup, leaving for a few seconds to lightly warm through. Remove strawberries and place on the shortbread. Serve immediately while the strawberries are still warm.

FRENCH STRAWBERRY FLAN (serves 6-8)

4ozs/125g plain flour
2ozs/50g butter
2ozs/60g castor sugar
2 egg yolks
2 drops of vanilla essence
12ozs/375g strawberries
3tbsp/45ml redcurrant jelly

To make the pastry, sieve the flour onto a pastry board and make a well in the centre. Place the butter, sugar, egg yolks and vanilla essence in the middle and using fingertips only, lightly work these ingredients gradually drawing in the flour, until well blended. Knead mixture lightly until it is smooth. Wrap in cling film and chill in a refrigerator for about an hour.

Set oven at 375F/190C/Gas Mark 5.

Roll out pastry and line the flan ring and bake blind for 15-20 minutes. Allow to cool and very carefully remove from tin. Hull the strawberries and arrange in the flan case. Heat the redcurrant jelly to make a glaze and brush over the arranged strawberries. Allow to cool before serving.

STRAWBERRY CHEEESECAKE (serves 8-10)

1½ozs/40g semi-sweet biscuits (crushed)
Pinch of ground mace
½ ounce/15g butter (melted)
4 large eggs (separated)
7ozs/175g castor sugar
1lb/500g soft cream cheese
1½ozs/40g plain flour
2tbsp/30ml lemon juice
½ pint/300ml whipped double cream
1lb/500g strawberries
6 tbsp/90ml redcurrant jelly
1tbsp/15ml arrowroot

Set oven at 250F/120C/Gas Mark ½

Mix the crushed biscuits with the ground mace, brush the melted butter over the base and sides of a loose-based 8"/20cm cake tin and dust over with the crumbs. Shake out excess. In a large bowl, whisk the egg yolks, add the sugar and continue beating until the mixture is thick and fluffy. Mash the cream cheese in a bowl until soft and beat into the egg yolk mixture with the flour, lemon juice and cream. Whisk the egg whites until stiff and fold into the cream cheese mixture. Pour into the prepared cake tin and bake for about one and a half hours. Turn off the oven and leave the cheesecake in the oven for two hours (do not open the door). Remove from oven and allow cake to cool in the tin.

Loosen the cake by pushing up the bottom of the tin and cut into three layers. Place bottom layer on a serving plate. Prepare the strawberries and halve them arranging a third over each of the three layers. Heat the redcurrant jelly in a small pan, blend the arrowroot with a little water and add a little of the jelly. Return mixture to pan with the remaining jelly, bring to the boil and cook until the jelly is thick and clear. Spoon some of the glaze over each of the three layers and on the top layer allow the remainder of the glaze to trickle down the sides of the cake. Leave it to set for 30 minutes before serving.

STRAWBERRY CHIFFON PIE (serves 6)

1 pastry pie shell as for Blackberry pie on page 64 baked blind
5ozs/150g strawberries
4ozs/100g sugar
1tbsp/15ml gelatine
2ozs/50g sugar
¼ pint/150ml water
1tbsp/15ml lemon juice
Pinch salt
2 egg whites

Wash and hull the strawberries, reserving a few good ones for decoration, and slice the remainder. Put the sliced strawberries in a bowl, cover with the sugar and leave to stand for half an hour. In a small saucepan mix the gelatine, sugar, water, lemon juice and salt and stir over a gentle heat until the gelatine dissolves. Pour over the strawberries, stirring well, and chill until the mixture begins to thicken. Whisk the egg whites and fold into the strawberry mixture. Pour into the pie shell and garnish with the reserved strawberries. Leave to chill before serving.

STRAWBERRY MERINGUE (serves 6)

4 egg whites
9ozs/275g icing sugar
2ozs/50g finely ground hazel nuts
1pt/600ml vanilla ice cream
1lb/500g strawberries (washed and hulled)
6tbsp/90ml raspberry jam

Set oven at 250F/130C/Gas Mark ½

Place baking or rice paper on a baking sheet. Put the egg whites in a large bowl, sift the icing sugar and add to the egg whites. Whisk the egg whites and sugar until a stiff mixture is formed. Carefully fold in the ground hazel nuts. Using a large star nozzle in a forcing bag, pipe a 7"-8"/18-20cm ring of meringue on the baking paper. Fill the centre with more meringue and pipe two more rings around the top edge to form a basket. Dust lightly with a little icing sugar. Bake for 3-4 hours - the meringue should be crisp and easy to handle but do not allow it to become too dry. Place on a serving dish. Sieve the jam and add a little water to make a thin syrup. Fill the meringue basket with the ice cream and cover with the prepared strawberries. Spoon over the jam syrup and serve immediately.

STRAWBERRY BLITZ TORTE

4ozs/125g butter
4ozs/125g castor sugar
1tsp vanilla or almond essence
4 egg yolks
4ozs/125g sifted plain flour
1tsp/5ml baking powder
4fl.ozs/125ml milk
5 egg whites
Pinch of cream of tartar
12ozs/375g strawberries
Whipped cream

Set oven at 250F/120C/Gas Mark ½.

Butter two 8"-9"/20-23cm sponge tins, line the bottoms with baking paper and butter the paper lightly. Cream the butter until light and fluffy and beat in the sugar, essence and egg yolks, one at a time. Mix the flour and baking powder and with the milk add to the creamed mixture alternately. Spread the mixture in the baking tins. Beat the egg whites and cream of tartar until stiff and spread evenly over the yolk mixture. Bake for 25 minutes in the cool oven and then increase the temperature to 350F/180C/Gas Mark 4 and bake for a further 20 minutes. Remove from the oven and leave to cool. Crush the strawberries and spread over the bottom layer with a little cream. Place the other layer on top and decorate or cover with cream as desired. Serve immediately.

CRISPY STRAWBERRY FLAN (serves 4)

12ozs/375g crushed digestive biscuits
6ozs/175g butter
3tbsp/45ml honey or golden syrup
3-4 ripe pears
A little lemon juice
1 small can mandarin oranges
8ozs/250g strawberries (hulled and washed)

Glaze -
3tbsp/45ml honey or golden syrup
1oz/25g castor sugar
1tbsp/15ml syrup from the canned oranges

Melt the butter in a large saucepan, add the honey or golden syrup and stir in the biscuit crumbs. Press the mixture into the bottom and sides of a shallow pie dish and put in a cool place to set. Peel and core the pears and sprinkle with a little lemon juice to prevent discolouration. Neatly arrange slices of pear and oranges around the edge of the flan and fill the centre with whole or halved strawberries. To make the glaze put the honey or golden syrup in a small pan with the sugar and orange syrup and heat gently until the sugar has dissolved. Spoon carefully over the fruit and chill. Serve with whipped cream.

Puddings

BERRY COBBLER (serves 4)

1lb/500g blackberries, loganberries or blueberries
6ozs/175g sugar
1 egg (well beaten) or ½ ounce/15g flour

For the topping -
6ozs/175g plain flour
2tsp baking powder
Pinch of salt
4ozs/125g sugar
1 egg
4fl.ozs/120ml milk
4ozs/125g butter (melted)

Set oven at 400F/200C/Gas Mark 6.

Prepare the fruit, add the sugar and egg or flour and arrange in a well buttered deep pie dish. To make the topping, put the flour, baking powder, salt and sugar in a bowl and mix well. In a separate bowl, beat together the egg, milk and melted butter and stir gently into the flour mixture. Pour mixture over the fruit and bake for 20-25 minutes when it should be brown and crusty. Serve hot with custard or cream.

BLACKBERRY & APPLE CRUMBLE (serves 4-6)

3ozs/75g butter or margarine
6ozs/175g self raising flour
3ozs/75g demerara sugar
1lb/500g cooking apples (peeled, cored and sliced)
8ozs/250g blackberries
3ozs/75g sugar

Set oven at 350F/180C/Gas Mark 4.

Rub the fat into the flour until the mixture has a "breadcrumb" texture and stir in the demerara sugar. Well grease a deep ovenproof dish and arrange layers of the apple, blackberries and sugar in the dish. Cover the fruit completely with the crumble mixture and than bake for 40-45 minutes until the top is golden brown. Best served hot with vanilla ice cream, cream or custard.

REDCURRANT AND ORANGE PUDDING (serves 4)

15ozs/450g redcurrants with stalks removed
2 medium oranges
1oz/25g sugar
2ozs/50g fresh breadcrumbs
2 eggs

Set oven at 325F/160C/Gas Mark 3.

Squeeze the juice out of the oranges and put in a small saucepan with the prepared redcurrants. Cook gently over a low heat for about 10 minutes or until the currants are soft. Add the sugar and adjust to taste. Press the cooked redcurrants through a sieve, extracting as much juice as possible and stir into the breadcrumbs. Lightly beat the eggs and add to the redcurrant mixture and beat well. Lightly grease four ramekin dishes and spoon the mixture into them. Stand the ramekins in a roasting tin and pour hot water around them until just under half way up the dishes. Bake for 30-35 minutes when the puddings should be just set. Serve hot or cold.

BLACKCURRANT & APPLE SCONE PUDDING

8ozs/250g blackcurrants (with stalks removed)
8ozs/250g peeled, cored and sliced apples
4ozs/125g sugar
2tbsp/30ml water

For the scone mix -
6ozs/175g plain flour
2tsp/10ml baking powder
2ozs/50g butter
Milk to mix

Put the fruit, sugar and water in a large frying pan until it is heated through and the juice is beginning to run. Put the flour and baking powder in a bowl and rub in the butter, then gradually add enough milk to form a stiff paste. Lightly flour a pastry board and roll out the mixture to about half inch/10mm thick and cut into 1"/2.5cm squares. Lay scones on top of the fruit mixture, cover pan and simmer very gently for about 15 minutes. The scone should rise and soak up the fruit juices. Serve hot with cream.

CURRANT PUDDING

8ozs/250g red or blackcurrants
1lb/500g stale bread
2pts/1200ml milk
6ozs/175g sugar
4 eggs
1tbsp/15ml rum

Set oven at 350F/180C/Gas Mark 4.

Put the milk and sugar in a saucepan and bring to the boil. Meanwhile put the breadcrumbs in a large bowl and pour over the sweetened milk. Leave to stand for 10 minutes and then pass mixture through a sieve. Put the beaten eggs, fruit and rum in a bowl and mix in the bread mixture. Pour mixture into a lightly buttered oven proof dish and bake for about an hour. May be served hot or cold.

TAPIOCA AND REDCURRANT PUDDING

2ozs/50g tapioca
1pt/600ml milk
Vanilla essence
Sugar to taste
1lb/500g redcurrants with stalks removed
6ozs/175g sugar
Pinch of cinnamon
A little water

Put the tapioca and milk in a double saucepan and boil until all the milk has been absorbed. Add the vanilla essence and sugar to taste ensuring the sugar is dissolved. Cook the redcurrants gently in a little water and sugar until soft. Spoon the redcurrants into a serving dish, pour the cooked tapioca over the top and sprinkle with cinnamon.

GOOSEBERRY BREAD PUDDING (serves 4)

6ozs/175g gooseberries (topped and tailed)
1lb/500g stale bread
2pts/1200ml milk
4 eggs
1tbsp/15ml rum
4ozs/125g sugar

Set oven at 350F/180C/Gas Mark 4.

Put the milk and sugar in a saucepan and bring to the boil. Meanwhile put the breadcrumbs in a large bowl and pour over the sweetened milk. Leave to stand for 10 minutes and then pass mixture through a sieve. Put the beaten eggs, fruit and rum in a bowl and mix in the bread mixture. Pour mixture into a lightly buttered oven proof dish and bake for about an hour. May be served hot or cold.

STEAMED GOOSEBERRY PUDDING (serves 4)

8ozs/250g self-raising flour
Pinch salt
2-4ozs/60-125g shredded suet
Cold water to mix
1lb/500g gooseberries (topped and tailed)
6ozs/175g sugar

Sieve the flour and salt and stir in the suet. Gradually add the cold water to form a soft dough. Roll out thinly on a floured board and line a well greased basin with two-thirds of the suet pastry. Fill the inside with the gooseberries and sugar and cover with a lid of the pastry. Cover the top with greaseproof paper and tie on a pudding cloth, allowing room for the crust to rise. Steam for about 2 - 2½ hours and serve hot with custard or cream.

Black or redcurrants make an equally delicious pudding.

SUMMER PUDDING (serves 6-8)

1lb/500g mixed summer fruits (red or blackcurrants, blackberries, etc)
4ozs/125g castor sugar
8ozs/250g raspberries
8 slices of white bread with crusts removed

Cook the mixed summer fruits with the sugar for about 10-15 minutes until they are tender. Add the raspberries, leave fruit to cool and then strain, reserving the juice. Line a pudding basin with some of the bread and reserve 2 slices cut into circles to fit the top of the basin. Pour half the fruit into the basin and place a circle of bread on top. Pour over the remaining fruit and top with the remaining bread circle. Cover the top with a saucer small enough to fit inside the basin and place a weight on top. Leave in a refrigerator overnight. When ready to serve turn out on to a serving plate and pour over any remaining fruit juice. Serve with cream.

Individual summer puddings can be made by using small basins and dividing the ingredients equally.

SUMMER CRUMBLE

4ozs/125g plain flour
2ozs/50g margarine
1oz/25g castor sugar
1tsp/5ml mixed spice
1lb/500g mixed summer fruits (red or blackcurrants, blackberries, raspberries, etc)

Set oven at 400F/200C/Gas Mark 6.

Put the flour in a bowl and rub in the margarine. Add the sugar and mixed spice and mix well. Put the mixed fruits in a lightly buttered ovenproof dish and spoon over the crumble mixture. Bake for about 20-25 minutes or until golden brown. Serve hot with cream or yoghurt.

WHIPPED FRUIT PUDDING (serves 4)

15fl.ozs/450ml orange juice
1tbsp/15ml arrowroot
3tbsp/45ml maple syrup or 2tbsp/30ml clear honey
Juice of half a lemon
8ozs/250g mixed raspberries and strawberries (hulled)
1/4 pint/150ml whipped double cream or yoghurt

Put the orange juice in a pan and heat. Blend a little of the warmed juice with the arrowroot, return mixture to the pan and bring to the boil to thicken, stirring continuously. Pour mixture into a bowl and whisk until light and fluffy, then add the maple syrup or honey and lemon juice, continuing to whisk. Set aside a few whole fruits for decoration and mash the remainder. Fold into the whisked syrup with cream or yoghurt. Pour into individual dishes and leave to chill, decorating with the reserved fruits when ready to serve.

RASPBERRY PUDDING

6ozs/175g raspberries
6ozs/175g sugar
8ozs/250g stale bread
2ozs/50g butter
3 eggs
15fl.ozs/450ml milk
1tbsp/15ml rum

Set oven at 350F/180C/Gas Mark 4.

Boil the milk with the sugar and pour over the bread. Leave to stand for 10 minutes and then pass through a sieve. Add the butter and beaten eggs, mix well and then stir in the fruit and rum. Pour mixture into a lightly buttered ovenproof dish and bake for about an hour. Serve hot with cream or custard.

QUICK RASPBERRY RICE PUDDING (serves 6)

1x13ozs/370g tin of raspberries
2tbsp/30ml mixed fruit jam
2 med or 1 large can of rice pudding

Put the fruit and jam in food processor and blend until smooth. Press mixture through a sieve to remove the pips. Pour the rice pudding into a saucepan and allow to simmer gently for 2-3 minutes, stirring occasionally. Spoon rice pudding into individual serving dishes and pour over the fruit sauce.
Serve immediately.

Sauces

CURRANT SAUCE (serves 4)

8ozs/250g redcurrants with stalks removed
8ozs/250g blackcurrants with stalks removed
3tbsp/45ml water
1tsp/5ml arrowroot
½ ounce/15g sugar

Put the fruit in a saucepan with the water, cover and place over a low heat for about ten minutes until the currants are well cooked. Press the cooked fruit through a sieve. Blend the arrowroot with a little water to make a smooth paste. Pour the purée into a clean saucepan, add the sugar and arrowroot paste and bring to the boil, stirring continuously. Continue to boil the sauce until it is thick enough to coat the back of the spoon. Use hot or cold.

FRESH PEACHES IN BLACKCURRANT SAUCE (serves 6)

1lb/500g blackcurrants with stalks removed
4ozs/125g castor sugar
8fl.ozs/250ml water
Grated rind and juice of 1 orange
6 ripe peaches (peeled)

Put the fruit, sugar and water in a pan, bring to the boil and simmer gently until the fruit is soft. Press the fruit through a sieve and then add the orange rind and juice. Arrange the peaches in a serving bowl and pour over the blackcurrant sauce. Leave to chill and serve with whipped double cream.

GOOSEBERRY SAUCE

1lb/500g gooseberries
4ozs/125g sugar
1tbsp/15ml water

Put fruit, sugar and water in a saucepan, bring to the boil and simmer until the gooseberries are soft. Leave to cool and then press through a sieve. Set aside purée until ready to serve.

RASPBERRY SAUCE

2lbs/1kg raspberries
1tbsp/15ml arrowroot
2tsp/10ml orange or lemon juice
3ozs/75g sugar

Put the raspberries in a food processor to reduce to a purée and then press through a sieve to remove the pips. Mix the arrowroot with a little of the raspberry juice and set aside. Pour the remaining juice into a saucepan, add the sugar and orange or lemon juice and heat slowly to dissolve the sugar, stirring constantly. Bring mixture just to boiling point, remove from heat and stir in the arrowroot mixture. Return pan to a lower heat and allow mixture to simmer. Continue stirring while mixture thickens which will take about 2 minutes. Leave sauce to cool to room temperature and use as desired.

STRAWBERRY HARD SAUCE

6ozs/200g strawberries (hulled and washed)
3ozs/100g butter
4ozs/125g icing sugar
Few drops of vanilla essence
1 egg white

Allow the butter to soften and cream with a wooden spoon. Gradually beat in the sugar and vanilla essence a drop at a time. Break down the egg white and beat into the butter and sugar mixture. Press the strawberries through a sieve and add the resultant purée to the sugar mixture. The sauce may be used at room temperature or chilled.

RHUBARB AND BERRY SAUCE

8ozs/250g rhubarb
8ozs/250g strawberries (hulled)
4ozs/125g sugar
Juice and finely grated rind of 1 lemon

Wash the rhubarb, cut into 2"/5cm pieces and place in a saucepan. Cover with water and cook over a moderate heat for about 10 minutes or until tender. Strain the rhubarb through a sieve and discard the liquid. Take out a few strawberries for decoration and put the remainder with the rhubarb, sugar, lemon rind and juice into a food processor to purée. Press the purée through a sieve to remove any seeds and stringy pieces of rhubarb. Place in a dish, cover and put to chill until needed. When ready to serve, decorate with sliced strawberries and serve with ice cream or crepes.

STRAWBERRY CREAM SAUCE

1 egg separated
4ozs/125g icing sugar
8ozs/250g mashed strawberries
4fl.ozs/120ml double cream
2fl.ozs/60ml milk

Beat the egg white until stiff and then beat the egg yolk. Stir into the egg white and gradually add the remaining ingredients blending well. Put in a cool place until ready to serve - ideal with squares of sponge cake or sliced swiss roll.

Salads

CURRANT SALAD IN ORANGE BASKETS (serves 6)

6 oranges
1lb/500g mixed red and white currants (destalked)
1oz/25g castor sugar
1tbsp/15ml maraschino
1tbsp/15ml kirsch

Using a small knife cut off the tops, leaving a small strip to form a handle, and scoop out the flesh with a small spoon. Wash and drain the basket. Put the currants in a bowl, stir in the sugar and pour over the maraschino and kirsch. If quantity looks a little small, stir in a little of the orange flesh. Leave the fruit to marinate for about half an hour and then fill the baskets with the fruit mixture.

CURRANT AND RASPBERRY SALAD (serves 4)

8ozs/250g mixed white and redcurrants (destalked)
8ozs/250g raspberries
2ozs/50g castor sugar
2tbs/30ml maraschino

Put the fruit in a bowl with the sugar and maraschino. Shake the bowl gently instead of stirring with a spoon so as not to bruise the fruit. Leave to chill before serving.

FRUIT SALAD BOWL

As many fresh fruits as possible may be used for this - white and black grapes, peaches, apricots, oranges in quarters, white and red currants, strawberries, raspberries, cherries and pineapple.

Remove pips from grapes. Remove stalks from strawberries, raspberries amd currants. Take stone out of apricots and peaches and cut fruit into quarters. Stone the cherries and cut the pineapple into equal pieces. Skin the oranges, removing all the pith and pips, and dividing them into quarters.

Put all the fruit in a large bowl and sprinkle over with castor sugar, adjust to your taste, and pour over 2 tablespoons each of maraschino and kirsch.
Do not stir fruit with a spoon but shake the bowl to "marinate" the fruit.
Leave to chill before serving.

STRAWBERRY AND CHICKEN RICE (serves 6-8)

8ozs/250g long grain rice
Pinch of salt
4ozs/125g frozen peas
8ozs/250g cooked chicken
8ozs/250g small strawberries (hulled)
6tbsp/90ml mayonnaise
Pepper

Cook the rice as instructed, drain and rinse under cold water. Cook the peas and rinse under cold water. Cut the chicken into small pieces and mix it with the rice and peas. Cut the strawberries into halves or quarters, depending on their size, and mix carefully into the rice with the mayonnaise and salt and pepper. Leave in a cool place until ready to serve.

MELON WITH STRAWBERRIES

1 ripe melon
4ozs/125g castor sugar
2tbsp/30ml sherry
8ozs/250g strawberries

Cut the top off the melon and scoop out the seeds. Carefully remove the flesh with a spoon, cut into small pieces and place in a bowl with half the sugar and cover with the sherry. Remove stalks from the strawberries and if necessary cut up so they are all about the same size. Place in a bowl, sprinkle over the remaining sugar and leave for about quarter of an hour. Mix together the melon and strawberries with their juices and put into the melon. Leave to chill until ready to serve.

PINEAPPLE AND STRAWBERRY SALAD

1 pineapple
Sugar and water to make a thin syrup
4ozs/125g castor sugar
2tbsp/30ml maraschino
8ozs/250g good strawberries
1 glass of white wine

Cut away outer skin from the pineapple, cut into thin slices and then cut in half again and remove the centre core with a round cutter. Blanch slices for about 5 minutes in a thin syrup (sugar dissolved in water and left to cool), drain and then place in the maraschino and half the castor sugar.

Remove stalks from the strawberries and put in a bowl with the remaining sugar and pour over the glass of white wine. Lightly stir the fruit, taking care not to bruise it and then leave for ten minutes.

Arrange the slices of pineapple around the edge of a serving dish and fill the middle with the strawberries. Mix the syrups and spoon over the strawberries and leave to chill until ready to serve.

CHANTILLY STRAWBERRIES

1lb/500g strawberries
Juice of 1 lemon
2tbsp/30ml kirsch or liqueur of your choice
1oz/25g castor sugar
½ pint/300ml double cream
A few drops of vanilla essence

Wash and remove stalks from the strawberries. Put them in a bowl, pour over the lemon juice and kirsch and sprinkle over the sugar. Leave to steep for about half an hour. Whip the cream with the vanilla essence. Serve the fruit in a glass dish with the whipped cream.

WILD STRAWBERRY SALAD

Use small or wild strawberries for this salad. Remove stalks, wash the strawberries and place in a bowl with sugar, to your taste, and a glass or two of white or red wine (depending on the quantity of strawberries).
Stir carefully to mix the wine and sugar and then turn on to a fruit dish.

CUCUMBER AND STRAWBERRY SALAD (serves 4)

Half a cucumber
Salt
8ozs/250g ripe strawberries
2 fresh ripe figs
3tbsp/45ml sunflower oil
1tbsp/15ml balsamic or wine vinegar
Freshly ground black pepper

Score the skin of the cucumber lengthways with a fork and cut into thin slices. Place slices on a plate and sprinkle over the salt.
Leave to stand for 30 minutes.

Remove stalks from the strawberries and wipe the figs. Reserve a few strawberries for decoration. Slice the remaining strawberries in half lengthways and the figs into quarters. To make the dressing, whisk together the oil, vinegar and pepper.

Drain the cucumber, pat dry with absorbent kitchen paper and arrange on a serving plate with the strawberries and figs. Sprinkle over the prepared dressing and garnish with the reserved strawberries. Serve while still fresh.

Preserves & Jams

A few tips which may help when making jam or preserves.

1. Before using, all containers should be washed in hot, soapy water and rinsed thoroughly in hot water. Dry containers in a warm oven and handle them as little as possible.

2. There are two ways to test for setting point -
   a) by using a sugar thermometer which should be dipped in hot water before being used to test the jam. Submerge the thermometer bulb completely and setting point is reached when the thermometer registers 105C/221F.
   b) by using a cold plate. Pour a small amount of the jam on a cold plate and leave to stand until it is cold. Run your finger across the top and if the surface wrinkles, it is ready. If it is not ready, return to the heat for about five minutes before repeating the test. When ready, remove jam from the heat immediately.

3. Wipe the rim of the containers with a damp cloth before placing a waxed disc on the top of the contents and then covering with a top or cellophane secured with a rubber band.

4. Always store preserves and jams in a cool, dark place.

RASPBERRY JAM

2lbs/900g raspberries
1lb8ozs/750g sugar

Put the sugar to warm in the oven.

Put the raspberries in a heavy based saucepan, crush them with a masher and then cook for about 15 minutes to reduce the liquid. Add the warmed sugar and keep stirring to prevent the jam from sticking. Skim off the scum which may form on the top and test for setting. Put into clean, warm jars and seal.

NB. Blackberries may be used but you may wish to put the cooked mixture through a sieve to remove the pips.

BLACKBERRY & APPLE JAM

1lb/500g sliced cooking apples
4tbsp/60ml water
1lb/500g blackberries (washed)
2lbs/1kg sugar

Put the apples and water in a heavy based pan and cook gently until the apples are soft. Add the blackberries and continue cooking until all the fruit is soft. Stir in the sugar and continue stirring until it is all dissolved. Boil the jam briskly until setting point is reached and then remove from heat. Skim off any scum which may have formed and leave to cool a short while before pouring into clean, warmed jars. Cover and seal.

BLACKBERRY CHUTNEY

1lb/500g cooking apples
12ozs/375g onions
3lbs/$1\frac{1}{2}$kgs blackberries (washed)
2tsp powdered ginger
1tsp powdered mace
$\frac{1}{2}$ ounce/10g mustard
3tsp/10g salt
1pt/600ml white vinegar
1lb/500g brown sugar

Peel and chop the apples and onions and put in a large heavy based pan with the blackberries, spices, seasoning and $\frac{1}{4}$ pint/150ml of the vinegar. Bring to the boil and cook for about an hour, stirring frequently and gradually adding the remainder of the vinegar. Rub the cooked mixture through a sieve to remove the pips, add the sugar and stir until it is quite dissolved. Allow mixture to simmer until the required consistency is achieved. Pour into clean, warmed jars and seal when cold.

BLACKBERRY JELLY

1lb/500g blackberries (washed)
4tbsp/60ml water
1 med cooking apple (peeled, cored and sliced) or juice of 1 lemon
Sugar

Put the blackberries, water and apple (if using) into a pan and simmer until soft. Put the cooked pulp through a jelly bag and weigh the juice extracted. To every 1pt/600ml of juice allow 1lb/500g sugar. Put the juice in a pan with the sugar, add the lemon juice if using instead of the apple, and stirring continuously, bring to the boil. Continue to boil the mixture rapidly until setting point is reached. Pour into clean, warmed jars, cover and seal.

SPICED BRAMBLE JELLY

Set the oven at 275F/140C/Gas Mark 1.

For every 1lb/500g blackberries allow 1tsp mixed spice.

Weigh and wash the fruit and put in a covered heatproof dish with the mixed spice. Place in the oven and bake until the fruit is tender and the juice is beginning to exude. Put the cooked fruit in a jelly bag, leave to drip overnight and squeeze the bag to ensure as much juice is extracted as possible. Measure the quantity of juice and for every 1pt/600ml allow 1lb/500g sugar. Warm the sugar and add it to the juice in a preserving pan. Gradually heat until the sugar is dissolved, stirring continuously, and bring to the boil. Allow the mixture to boil rapidly until it gels. Pour the jelly into clean, warmed jars, leave to cool and then cover.

BLUEBERRY & APPLE JELLY

3lbs/1½kg blueberries (stems removed)
3lbs/1½kg cooking apples (peeled, cored and coarsely chopped)
Juice of 2 lemons
Sugar

Put the blueberries and apple in a heavy based pan and just cover with water. Bring to the boil and simmer until the fruit is soft. Crush the berries with a wooden spoon and then strain through a jelly bag with the apple. Measure the juice and for every 1pt/600ml of juice allow 1lb/500g sugar. Return the juice to the saucepan and cook over a low heat. Add the lemon juice and sugar, stirring continuously until it is dissolved. Turn up the heat and boil rapidly until the jelly reaches 221F/105C. Remove from the heat and skim off any scum that may have formed. Pour into clean, warmed jars, cover and seal.

REDCURRANT JELLY

6lbs/2½kg redcurrants
Preserving sugar
2pts/120ml water

Wash the redcurrants but do not remove stalks. Put the fruit in a large preserving pan with the water, bring to the boil and simmer gently for about 40 minutes when the currants should be really soft. Using a jelly bag or 2/3 layers of muslin, strain the mixture, allowing it to drip through gradually. If there is quite a lot of fruit pulp left it can be returned to the pan with a further half pint/300ml of water, simmered and strained. Add the two juices together if you do this and measure. For every 1pt/600ml of juice allow 1lb/500g sugar. Return the juice to the pan, heating slowly and stirring continuously whilst adding the sugar. Continue to stir until all the sugar is dissolved and then bring rapidly to the boil. Boil briskly until setting point has been reached and then pour into warm, clean jars, cover and seal.

Alternatively you can make a mixed currant jelly by using equal quantities of red and blackcurrants.

REDCURRANT & LOGANBERRY JELLY

8ozs/250g redcurrants
8ozs/250g loganberries
1/2 pint/300ml water
Sugar

Wash the fruit and put in a pan with the water. Simmer gently and then strain the cooked fruit through a jelly bag. Leave it to drain overnight. Measure the liquid and for every 1pt/600ml allow 1lb/500g sugar. Return the juice to the pan and put over a low heat. Gradually add the sugar, stirring continuously until it is dissolved. Bring rapidly to the boil and allow to boil until setting point is reached. Pour into clean, warmed jars, cover and seal.

SPICED CURRANTS

1lb.8ozs/750g currants
1lb/500g brown sugar
4fl.ozs/120ml mild cider vinegar
Small piece of cinnamon stick or 1tsp ground cinnamon
1tsp powdered cloves
1tsp allspice (if liked)

Remove the stems from the currants and wash. Put all the ingredients in a large heavy-based saucepan, bring to the boil and cook slowly for about an hour. Remove the cinnamon stick and serve hot or cold.

BLACKCURRANT SYRUP

6lbs/2.7kg blackcurrants
1pt/600ml water
Sugar

You will need 5-6x8fl.ozs/250ml bottles for the syrup and they should be washed and rinsed thoroughly and kept hot until needed.

Remove stems from the blackcurrants and put fruit in a large heavy based saucepan with the water. Bring to the boil and simmer gently for an hour. Crush the blackcurrants thoroughly and then strain through a jelly bag overnight. Measure the juice and for every 1pt/600ml allow 12ozs/375g sugar. Put the juice and sugar in the saucepan and warm over a low heat, stirring continuously until the sugar is dissolved. Increase the heat and bring to the boil without stirring.

Strain the hot syrup into one bottle up to within half an inch/1.5cm of the top. Wipe the bottles and cover. Place bottles in a saucepan, release the lids about half a turn and surround the bottles with boiling water for 30 minutes. Remove the bottles and tighten the lids immediately.

BLACKCURRANT JAM

1lb/500g blackcurrants
15fl.ozs/450ml water
1lb.2ozs/550g sugar

Wash currants and remove stalks. Place in a heavy-based saucepan with the water and simmer until fruit is quite soft. Stir in the sugar until it is quite dissolved, bring to the boil and cook rapidly until setting point is reached. Pour into clean, warmed jars, wipe rims and sides of jars, cover jam and seal.

BLACKCURRANT AND APPLE JAM

4lbs/2kgs blackcurrants (with stalks removed)
½ pint/300ml water
1lb.8ozs/750g cooking apples (peeled, cored and sliced)
6lbs/3kgs granulated sugar

Wash the blackcurrants and put in a preserving pan with half the water. Bring to the boil and allow to simmer until tender. Put the apples in another pan with the remaining water and cook until soft. Combine the two fruits in one pan, add the sugar and heat gently, stirring continuously until the sugar is dissolved. Bring to the boil and cook rapidly until setting point is reached (you should allow about 15 minutes). Remove the scum and pour into clean, warmed jars. Cover and seal.

GOOSEBERRY CATSUP

2lbs/1kg gooseberries
1lb/500g brown sugar
4fl.ozs/120ml mild cider vinegar
Small piece of cinnamon stick or 1tsp ground cinnamon
1tsp powdered cloves
1tsp allspice (if liked)

Top and tail the gooseberries and put fruit in a large heavy-based saucepan. Add the remaining ingredients, bring to the boil and cook slowly for two hours. Remove the cinnamon stick if used and allow mixture to cool slightly before pouring into clean, warmed jars. Leave to cool and then seal.

GOOSEBERRY AND ORANGE JAM

1lb.8ozs/750g gooseberries
5fl.ozs/150ml water
Juice and grated rind of 2 oranges
1lb.8ozs/750g sugar

Top, tail and wash the gooseberries, put them in a large heavy-based pan and cook them with the water, orange juice and rind until soft. Add the sugar and stir until it is completely dissolved. Bring to the boil and cook rapidly until setting point is reached. Pour into clean, warmed jars, cover and seal.

GOOSEBERRY RELISH

2lbs/1kg gooseberries (topped, tailed and washed)
10ozs/300g seeded raisins
1 onion (peeled and sliced)
6ozs/375g brown sugar
1ozs/25g dried mustard
1ozs/25g ginger
1ozs/25g salt
1/4 teaspoon cayenne
1tsp turmeric (if to your taste)
2pts/1200ml vinegar

Put the gooseberries, raisins and onion in a food processor and chop finely. Put the chopped mixture in a large saucepan and add the remaining ingredients. Bring slowly to the boil and then cook for 45 minutes. Strain cooked mixture through a coarse sieve into clean, warmed jars and leave to cool before sealing.

GOOSEBERRY JAM

10lbs/5kgs gooseberries
6lbs/3kgs sugar
2pts/1200ml water
Juice of 1 lemon

Top and tail and wash the gooseberries. Put the sugar and water in a large saucepan and heat gently until the sugar is dissolved. Then add the fruit and lemon juice and boil for about an hour. Pour into clean, warmed jars, cover and seal.

GOOSEBERRY JELLY

10lbs/5kgs gooseberries
1 lemon
A few drops of vanilla essence
Sugar

Wash the gooseberries and then crush them. Put the mashed fruit in a pan and boil for about 5 minutes. Pass through a sieve to remove the pips and weigh the juice. Add the same weight of sugar to the juice and return to the pan. Add the lemon juice and vanilla and cook for 15 minutes. Pour into clean, warmed jars, cover and seal.

STRAWBERRY AND GOOSEBERRY JELLY

1lb/500g gooseberries
5fl.ozs/150ml water
1lb/500g strawberries
Sugar
Lemon juice

Wash the gooseberries and put in a pan with the water. Cook until fruit is nearly soft and then add the washed strawberries. Continue cooking until both fruits are very soft.
Put the cooked fruits through a jelly bag overnight and then weigh the strained juice. To every 1pt/600ml of juice allow 1lb/500g sugar. Put the juice, sugar and lemon juice in a pan and stirring continuously, heat gradually until the sugar dissolves. Then bring rapidly to the boil and cook briskly until setting point is reached. Put into clean, warmed pots, cover and seal.

MIXED FRUIT IN BRANDY

1lb/500g mixed berries (strawberries, raspberries, blueberries, gooseberries)
2lbs/1kg sugar
16fl.ozs/500ml brandy
1lb/500g mixed fruit (peaches, plums, nectarines, apricots)

Rinse and remove stalks from the berries and peel, remove stones and halve the fruit. In a large preserving jar put in a layer of the berries with some of the sugar and pour over enough brandy to cover. Then put a layer of the mixed fruit with some sugar and cover with some of the brandy. Continue in layers until fruit is about half an inch/1cm from the top of the jar. Seal and store in a cool dark place for at least two months before using.

MERRY JAM

1x8ozs/250g can crushed pineapple in syrup
1lb/500g dark sweet cherries
1lb/500g redcurrants (with stalks removed)
2 oranges (washed, thinly sliced and pips removed)
1lb/500g raspberries
Sugar

Drain the pineapple and reserve the syrup. Weigh all the prepared fruit, including the drained pineapple and allow 1lb/500g sugar for every 1lb/500g of fruit. Put the fruit in a large saucepan with the reserved syrup, add the sugar and heat slowly, stirring continuously, until the sugar is dissolved. Bring to the boil and cook rapidly for 15 minutes or until the mixture thickens. Ladle the jam into clean, warmed jars and wipe clean with a damp cloth. Cover and seal.

FRUIT BUTTER

1lb/500g blackcurrants
1lb/500g redcurrants
1lb/500g gooseberries
1lb/500g strawberries
2lbs/1kg sugar

Remove the stems from the currants, top and tail the gooseberries and remove the stalks from the strawberries. Put all the fruit in a large heavy-based pan and simmer until the juice begins to run. Increase the heat and cook for 15 minutes. Reduce the heat and gradually stir in the sugar until it is dissolved. Increase the heat again and boil rapidly for 25 minutes or until very thick.

Ladle the hot mixture into clean, warmed jars, wipe them clean and cover.

TIPSY FRUIT

Mixed fruit
Sugar
Rum

Equal quantities of good sound fruit such as strawberries, cherries, apricots, peaches, raspberries, plums, redcurrants, grapes or melon. Do not use citrus fruit, apples, pears or bananas.

Gently wipe the fruit but do not wash, peel or remove stones, except for the melon which should be peeled, seeded and cut into chunks. Weigh the fruit and allow equal amount of sugar. Layer the fruit and sugar in the jar and stir lightly. Pour rum over the fruit to cover. Seal and leave to mature in a cool dark place for three months. Fruit can always be added to the jar but allow equal quantity of sugar each time and cover with more rum.

Delicious served with cream, yoghurt or ice cream.

PEACH AND RASPBERRY JAM

2lbs/1kg peaches
5fl.ozs/150ml water
2tbsp/30ml lemon juice
2lbs/1kg raspberries
3lbs/1.4kg sugar

Peel and slice the peaches and remove stalks from the raspberries. Put the peaches in a large saucepan with the water and lemon juice and simmer until soft. Add the raspberries and simmer for 5 minutes. Gradually add the sugar, stirring continuously until it is dissolved, and increase the heat. Boil briskly for 15 to 20 minutes until jam reaches setting point or 221F/105C on a jam thermometer. Remove from heat and skim off the scum. Leave to cool for a few minutes and then ladle into clean, warm jars. Wipe jars and cover.

QUICK RASPBERRY JAM

1lb/500g raspberries
2tbsp/30ml lemon juice
1lb/500g sugar

Remove the stalks from the raspberries and put in a large microwave safe bowl. Add the sugar and lemon juice and stir lightly. Microwave on full power for 5 minutes, stirring occasionally until sugar dissolves. Microwave again on full power for 12 minutes or until jam reaches setting point or 221F/105C. Leave to stand for at least 5 minutes. Stir well and then ladle into clean, warm jars. Wipe jars with a damp cloth and cover.

RASPBERRY JELLY

4lbs/1.75kg raspberries
Sugar
1pt/600ml water

Wash the fruit, put in a pan with the water and simmer until soft. Place in a jelly bag and leave to drain overnight. Measure the juice and allow 1lb/500g sugar to 1pt/600ml of juice. Put the juice and sugar in a pan and heat slowly, stirring continuously, while the sugar dissolves. Bring to the boil and cook rapidly until setting point in reached. Pour into clean, warm jars, wipe clean with a damp cloth, cover and seal.

RASPBERRY COMPOTE

6lbs/2.7g raspberries
4lbs/1.8kg sugar

Put the raspberries and sugar in a pan and leave to stand for about one and half hours. Place the pan over heat and bring to the boil, simmering for 15 minutes. Place mixture into jars filling them up to only four-fifths and keep back one-fifth of the mixture. Leave all to cool. When cold, weigh the remaining one-fifth and add 7ozs/200g sugar to every 1lb/450g of fruit mixture. Bring to the boil and cook for 10 minutes and then fill up the jars over the less cooked compote.

RASPBERRY VINEGAR

1lb/500g ripe raspberries
1pt/600ml wine vinegar
2lbs/1kg sugar

Put raspberries in a earthenware jar and pour over the vinegar. Leave for four or five days and then pour out through a fine sieve, leaving the raspberries to drain for an hour. Put the liquid with the sugar in a pan and heat gently while the sugar dissolves. Bring to the boil and cook briskly until the quantity is reduced and slightly thickens. Pour into clean, warmed bottles and cover.

RASPBERRY SYRUP

1lb/500g raspberries
1lb/500g redcurrants
2lbs/1kg sugar

Use ripe fruit and crush through a fine sieve. Put the juice and sugar in a saucepan and bring to the boil. Allow it to boil for five minutes and remove from heat. Skim the juice, pour into a jug and allow to cool before bottling and covering.

PRESERVED RASPBERRIES

6lbs/3kgs raspberries
2lbs/1kg sugar
2pts/1200ml water

Put the fruit in a large bowl. Put the sugar and water in a large saucepan, heat gradually while the sugar dissolves and then boil for about three minutes. Pour the boiling syrup over the fruit and leave to stand for 15 minutes. Take the fruit out carefully with a draining spoon and place in clean jars. Return the juice to the heat and boil for another 15 minutes. Pour it over the fruit, wipe the edges of the jars and put the lids on. Place the jars in a pan with boiling water for about 20 minutes and then remove and leave to cool.

STRAWBERRY JELLY

1lb/500g strawberries
8ozs/250g redcurrants
2tbsp/30ml water
Sugar
Lemon juice

Wash the fruit and cook in the water until soft. Put the cooked mixture through a jelly bag, allowing sufficient time for it to drain thoroughly. Measure the juice and for every 1pt/600ml allow 1lb/500g sugar. Return the juice, sugar and lemon juice to the pan and heat gradually while the sugar dissolves, stirring constantly. Bring to the boil and cook rapidly until setting point is reached. Pour into clean, warmed jars, cover and seal.

QUICK STRAWBERRY JAM

1lb/500g strawberries
Juice of 1 lemon
11ozs/345g sugar
1tbsp/15ml butter

Wash, hull and slice the strawberries and place in a microwave bowl. Combine the lemon juice and sugar and cook for 20 minutes on high power, stirring occasionally. Check for setting. Stir in the butter until it is dissolved and leave to stand for half an hour before pouring into clean, warm jars. Seal tightly and store in a cool dark place.

STRAWBERRY JAM

3lbs/1.5kg strawberries
3lbs/1.5kg granulated sugar
8fl.ozs/250ml liquid pectin
Juice of 1 lemon

Remove stalks from the fruit and put in a large preserving pan with the lemon juice and sugar. Heat gently while the sugar dissolves, stirring continuously, add the pectin and then bring to the boil. Boil rapidly until setting point is reached, remove from heat and skim with a slotted spoon. Leave to cool for a few minutes before pouring into clean, warm jars. Cover and seal.

Gateaux & Cakes

BLUEBERRY MUFFINS

8ozs/250g plain flour
3tsp baking powder
Pinch of salt
2ozs/50g sugar
2 eggs
8fl.ozs/250ml milk
2oz/50g melted butter
8ozs/250g blueberries

Set oven at 400F/200C/Gas Mark 6.

Sift the flour, baking powder and salt into a bowl, reserving about a quarter of flour in a separate dish. In a separate bowl, beat the eggs, milk and melted butter together. Pour over the flour mixture and stir in lightly, do not overbeat. Prepare the fruit, sprinkle over the reserved flour and then stir into the muffin mixture. Spoon mixture into buttered muffin tins to about two-thirds full and bake for about 15 minutes.

BLUEBERRY CAKE

6ozs/175g plain flour
2tsp baking powder
Pinch of salt
2ozs/50g butter or margarine
3ozs/75g sugar
Few drops of vanilla essence
1 egg
4fl.ozs/125ml milk
8ozs/250g blueberries (with stalks removed)
1oz/25g sugar
½ teaspoon of cinnamon

Set oven at 350F/180C/Gas Mark 4.

Sift the flour, baking powder and salt into a bowl. Cream the butter or margarine until light and fluffy and then gradually add the sugar, essence and beaten egg. Stir in half the flour mixture and half the milk, blending thoroughly and then add the remainder of the flour and milk. Pour batter mixture into an 8"x8"/20x20cm lightly buttered pan and cover with the blueberries. Sprinkle over the sugar mixed with the cinnamon. Bake for about 25 minutes and cut into squares while still warm. Serve immediately.

BLUEBERRY PANCAKES

4fl.ozs/125ml milk
2tbsp/30ml melted butter
1 egg
4ozs/125g plain flour
2tsp baking powder
2ozs/50g sugar
Pinch of salt
6ozs/175g blueberries (if using canned, drain off the juice)

Beat together the milk, melted butter and egg. Sift the flour and baking powder and add to the milk mixture with the sugar and salt. Whisk briskly until mixture resembles double cream, adding a little more milk if necessary.
Add the fruit and cook pancakes over a moderate heat in a griddle or frying pan. Serve immediately.

FRUITY SPONGE FINGERS

3 eggs
4ozs/125g castor sugar
3ozs/75g plain flour
Pinch of salt
Icing sugar
12ozs/375g mixed soft fruit (with stalks removed and washed)
1oz/25g icing sugar
10fl.ozs/300ml fromage frais or cream

Set oven at 375F/190C/Gas Mark 5.

Whisk the egg and sugar with an electric mixer until the mixture is thick and creamy. Sift the flour and salt and fold into the whisked mixture. Line two baking trays with baking parchment and spread the cake mixture to a thickness of ¼"/6mm. Bake for 8-10 minutes or until golden brown and firm. Remove sponges carefully from the tins and cut into required size for the fingers. Leave to cool and dredge with icing sugar.

Mix the icing sugar into the fromage frais or cream. Place the sponge fingers in individual serving dishes, spoon over the fromage frais or cream and most of the fruit. Top with a second finger of sponge and sprinkle over the remaining fruit. Serve immediately.

ALMOND GATEAU WITH RASPBERRIES

4 eggs (separated)
7ozs/200g castor sugar
3½ozs/100g ground almonds
Grated rind and juice of half a lemon
3½ozs/100g semolina

For the icing -
2ozs/50g granulated sugar
5fl.ozs/150ml water
8ozs/250g icing sugar
Lemon flavouring

1lb/500g raspberries
Castor sugar (to taste)
Set oven at 375F/190C/Gas Mark 5.

Grease and line a 9"/23cm deep cake tin. Beat the egg yolks and sugar together until thick and creamy. Gradually work in the ground almonds and lemon rind and juice and then leave to stand for a few minutes. Whisk the egg whites until stiff and fold into the almond mixture with the semolina. Turn the mixture into the prepared cake tin and bake for about 50 minutes. Leave to cool.

To make the icing, dissolve the granulated sugar in the water, bring to the boil and boil steadily for 10 minutes. Remove the pan from the heat and leave to get quite cold. Add the icing sugar, a little at a time and beating well with a wooden spoon. Add the lemon flavouring. The icing should coat the back of the spoon and look glossy. Warm the pan on a very low heat, do not allow it to get too hot.

Place the cake on a serving dish and pour over the glace icing. Serve with the raspberries in a separate dish and sprinkled with castor sugar.

RASPBERRY SHORTCAKE

1lb/500g raspberries
3tbsp/45ml redcurrant jelly
3fl.ozs/100ml whipped double cream

For the shortcake -
4ozs/125g plain flour
3ozs/75g butter
1½ozs/40g icing sugar
1 egg yolk
Few drops of vanilla essence

To make the shortcake, sift the flour onto a board and make a well in the middle. Put the butter, icing sugar, egg yolk and essence in the middle and gradually draw in the flour to work into a smooth paste, using the fingertips. Chill pastry for 30 minutes.

Set the oven at 375F/190C/Gas Mark 5.

Roll out the pastry into a round about ¼"/6mm thick and 8"/20cm in diameter, slide onto a baking sheet and bake for about 15-20 minutes when it should be light in colour. Allow shortbread to cool and place on a serving plate. Cover with the prepared raspberries and brush with the redcurrant jelly which has been slightly warmed. Allow to cool, decorate with the cream or serve separately as desired.

RASPBERRY GATEAU (serves 6)

3 eggs (separated)
4ozs/125g castor sugar
Grated rind and juice of half a lemon
2ozs/50g semolina
1oz/25g ground almonds

To decorate -
½ pint/300ml whipped double cream
8ozs/250g raspberries
4tbsp/60ml redcurrant jelly
2tsp/10ml water
2ozs/50g blanched almonds (chopped and toasted)

Set oven at 350F/180C/Gas Mark 4.

Put the egg yolks, sugar, lemon rind and juice in a bowl and whisk until thick and smooth. Stir in the semolina and ground almonds. Whisk the egg whites until firm and fold into the mixture, using a metal spoon. Line, grease and flour an 8"/20cm sandwich tin and pour in the mixture. Bake for 35-40 minutes and turn onto a cake rack to cool.

Cut the cake in half and sandwich together with three-quarters of the cream. Arrange the raspberries on the top leaving a small border around the edge. Put the redcurrant jelly in a small saucepan with the water, heat until smooth and then use to glaze the raspberries and sides of the sponge. Coat the sides with the toasted almonds and decorate with the remaining cream.

STRAWBERRY ALMOND MERINGUE (serves 6)

3ozs/75g ground almonds
6ozs/150g castor sugar
3 egg whites
8ozs/250g coffee-flavoured glacé icing (see recipe for icing under Almond Gateau with Raspberries and substitute the flavouring - page 124)
8ozs/250g strawberries
5fl.ozs/150ml double cream
Few drops of vanilla essence

Set oven for 325F/160C/Gas Mark 3.

Mix the almonds and castor sugar together, passing through a sieve to ensure they are well blended. Whisk the egg whites until firm and fold into the almond and sugar mixture. Line a large baking sheet with non-stick kitchen paper and divide the meringue mixture in half to make two 6"/15cm rounds. Bake for about 50-60 minutes and then lift very carefully on to a cooling rack, peeling off the baking paper. When quite cold, coat one of the rounds with the glacé icing.

Remove stalks from the strawberries and slice, reserving a few for decoration. Dust the sliced fruit with a little castor sugar. Whip the cream with a teaspoon of castor sugar and the vanilla essence.

Put the plain meringue on a serving plate, spoon over the cream and cover with the sliced strawberries. Put the iced round on top and decorate with the reserved strawberries. Keep in a cool place until ready to serve.

CHOCOLATE & STRAWBERRY GATEAU

12ozs/375g plain chocolate
12ozs/375g strawberries (with stalks removed)
4ozs/50g sugar
5tbsp/75ml water
10fl.ozs/300ml whipped double cream

For the sponge -
1 egg
2ozs/50g castor sugar
1½ozs/40g plain flour
Pinch of salt

Grease, sugar and flour a 6"/15cm cake tin.

Break up the chocolate into a small bowl and set over hot water to soften until it is thick enough to spread. Line a larger cake tin 8"/20cm with foil and spread the inside and bottom of the case fairly thickly with the chocolate. Ensure the sides are well coated and leave to set for several hours.

To make the syrup put the sugar and water in small saucepan and heat gently until the sugar is dissolved. Bring to the boil and boil rapidly for 10 minutes. Allqw to cool and set aside in a screw-top jar until ready to use.

Set oven at 350F/180C/Gas Mark 4.

To make the sponge, break the egg into a bowl and stir in the sugar. Using an electric beater, whisk for about 8 minutes when the mixture should hold its shape. Sift the flour with the salt and fold into the whisked mixture quickly and lightly, using a metal spoon. Pour mixture into the smaller cake tin and bake for 15-20 minutes. Cool on a wire rack.

Carefully peel away the foil from the chocolate case, keeping your hand on the outside of the foil and not touching the chocolate. Split the sponge cake into two rounds and put one in the bottom of the chocolate case. Spoon over about half the syrup to well soak the sponge half. Slice the strawberries, reserving a few for decoration and arrange on top of the sponge. Moisten with a little of the syrup brushed over them. Cover with a layer of whipped cream and place the other sponge round on top. Spoon over the rest of the syrup and cover with the remaining cream. Decorate with the reserved strawberries and leave in a cool place until ready to serve.

WALNUT AND STRAWBERRY GATEAU (serves 6-8)

6ozs/175g butter or margarine
4ozs/125g castor sugar
Grated rind of half a lemon
6ozs/175g plain flour
4ozs/125g chopped walnuts

10fl.ozs/300ml whipping cream
1oz/25g icing sugar
1lb.8ozs/750g strawberries (hulled)

Set oven at 350F/180C/Gas Mark 4.

Lightly grease three baking trays. Cream the fat and sugar together until light and fluffy and then beat in the lemon rind and fold in the flour. Knead the mixture until it is smooth, wrap in cling film and place in a refrigerator for about half an hour. Divide the mixture into three portions and roll out into a 7"/17.5cm circle. Place on the baking trays and sprinkle over the chopped walnuts. Bake for 20-25 minutes until golden brown. Leave to cool slightly before placing on a wire rack.

Whip the cream with the icing sugar until it is firm. Slice the strawberries, reserving a few for decoration. Using about two-thirds of the cream, stir in the sliced fruit and use to sandwich the cake rounds. Spread the remaining cream on the top and decorate with the reserved strawberries. Leave to chill before serving.

STRAWBERRY SHORTCAKE (serves 6)

4ozs/125g butter
2ozs/50g castor sugar
4ozs/125g plain flour
2ozs/50g cornflour
8ozs/250g strawberries (hulled)
10fl.ozs/300ml whipped double cream
A little sifted icing sugar for dredging

Set oven at 350F/180C/Gas Mark 4.

Sift the flour and cornflour. Cream the butter and sugar together until soft and creamy and then stir in the sifted flours. Mix to make a firm dough, turn on to a floured surface and gently knead. Divide mixture in half and roll out each piece to make an 8"/20cm round. Place on a baking sheet and cook for about 20 minutes. Leave for a few minutes before marking one round into 6 portions. Carefully slide both rounds onto a wire rack to cool.

Slice the strawberries, reserving a few for decoration. Mix three-quarters of the cream with the sliced fruit and spread over the plain shortcake round. Break the other round into 6 portions and arrange on top. Sprinkle over with icing sugar and decorate with the remaining cream and reserved strawberries.

ANGEL CAKE WITH STRAWBERRIES AND CREAM

2ozs/50g plain flour
6ozs/175g castor sugar
6 egg whites
Pinch of salt
3/4 tsp of cream of tartar
3 drops of vanilla essence
2 drops of almond essence

To decorate -
15fl.ozs/450ml double cream
1tsp castor sugar
2-3 drops of vanilla essence
1lb/500g strawberries (hulled)

Set oven at 375F/190C/Gas Mark 5.

Sift the flour and half the sugar at least three times. Put the egg whites, cream of tartar and salt in a large dry bowl and whisk with an electric beater until the mixture is mousse-like. Add the remaining sugar a little at a time and the essences and continue beating until the mixture is stiff. Carefully fold in the sifted flour and sugar. Turn the mixture into a clean, dry cake tin and level the surface. Bake the cake for 30-35 minutes or until firm to the touch. Turn cake upside down on a wire rack to cool in the tin and leave until quite cold. The cake will then come out of the tin easily. Cut the sponge into three layers.

Slice most of the strawberries, reserving a few for decoration, and whip the cream with the castor sugar and essence. Spread each cake layer with the cream and sliced strawberries, finishing with a complete cover of whipped cream. Halve the remaining strawberries and use to decorate the gateau. Put in a cool place until ready to serve.

STRAWBERRY SLICE (serves 6-8)

1x13ozs/368g packet of puff pastry
1lb/500g strawberries (hulled)
10fl.ozs/300ml whipped double cream
1oz/25g sifted icing sugar
4tbsp/60ml redcurrant jelly
2tsp/10ml water
2ozs/50g chopped and toasted almonds

Divide pastry into three equal portions and roll out into a rectangle 6"x14"/15x35cm. Place on dampened baking paper, prick lightly with a fork and leave to chill for 15 minutes.

Set oven at 425F/220C/Gas Mark 7.

Bake pastry for about 12-15 minutes until golden, turn it over and cook for a further 5 minutes. Remove from oven and leave to cool on a wire rack. Trim the edges to neaten and reserve the crumbs.

Divide the strawberries in half, slice one half and halve the remainder. Fold the sliced fruit into the whipped cream with the icing sugar. Place one of the cooked pastry slices on a serving plate and spread over half the cream and strawberry mixture. Put the second pastry slice on top, cover with the remaining mixture and put the last pastry slice on top. Heat the redcurrant jelly with the water in a small saucepan and glaze the top of the last pastry slice. Arrange the halved strawberries on the top and glaze with the remaining dissolved jelly. Mix the pastry crumbs with the almonds and cover the sides of the slice. Leave to cool until ready to serve but not too long or the pastry will soften.

MERINGUE BASKETS (serves 8)

4 egg whites
Few drops of vanilla essence
9ozs/275g icing sugar

For the filling;
5fl.ozs/150ml whipped double cream
4ozs/125g strawberries
2tbsp/30ml redcurrant jelly

Set oven at 300F/150C/Gas Mark 2.

Whisk the egg whites until stiff and then whisk in the vanilla essence and sifted icing sugar, a little at a time. Place the bowl over a pan of gently simmering water and continue to whisk for about 5 minutes when the meringue should be very stiff. Place a sheet of non-stick baking paper on a baking sheet and place half the meringue in rounds of about 3"/75mm diameter. Put the remaining meringue in a piping bag with a large fluted nozzle and pipe round the edge of each base to form the baskets. Bake for 1-1.1/4 hours. Slide onto a wire rack to cool and then remove the paper.

Hull and wash the strawberries. Spoon a little of the whipped cream into each basket and arrange the strawberries on top. Warm the redcurrant jelly and use as a glaze over the strawberries. Serve as soon as possible with extra cream if desired.

RICH STRAWBERRY GATEAU

4ozs/125g plain flour
4 eggs
6ozs/175g castor sugar
Pinch of salt

For the filling -
1lb/500g strawberries
1oz/25g castor sugar
4ozs/125g plain chocolate
10fl.ozs/300ml whipped double cream
Few drops of vanilla essence

Set oven at 375F/190C/Gas Mark 5.

Grease, sugar and flour a 3pt/1.75l ring mould. Sift the flour with the salt into a bowl. Whisk the eggs and sugar with an electric beater until mixture is thick and frothy. Fold in the flour with a metal spoon and pour into the prepared ring mould. Bake for about 35-40 minutes and then leave to cool on a wire rack.

Hull the strawberries and cut one-third of them into thick slices, covering with the castor sugar. Leave for 10-15 minutes and then press through a sieve to make a purée. Break up the chocolate into a small bowl and place over a pan of hot water to melt.

Cut the cake across to make three layers and place the bottom layer on a serving plate. Spread each layer with a thin coating of the melted chocolate and leave to set. Mix the strawberry purée with one-third of the whipped cream and spread this over the chocolate covered sponge layers. Sandwich them together. Add the vanilla essence to the remaining cream and a little sugar if desired. Spread over the cake and pile the rest of the strawberries in the middle. Leave in a cool place until ready to serve.

STRAWBERRY BABAS

4ozs/125g plain flour
½ ounce/15g yeast
1tbsp/15ml warm water
1 egg
½ ounce/15g castor sugar
Pinch of salt
2ozs/50g melted cooking fat

For the syrup -
5fl.ozs/150ml water
2ozs/50g sugar

To decorate -
8ozs/250g strawberries (hulled and washed)
A little whipped cream

To make the babas, sieve the flour into a warmed bowl and make a well in the centre. Put the yeast and warm water in the middle of the flour and mix together with a wooden spoon, drawing in about a quarter of the flour. Dust over the top with a little flour and place in a warm place, covered with a damp cloth, for about 15 minutes, when the yeast should start to show through the flour. Beat the egg and add to the flour with the sugar, salt and melted fat. Beat the ingredients thoroughly and again cover bowl with a damp cloth and leave in a warm place for about 45 minutes. The quantity should have doubled by then.

Divide the dough into 8 portions and place in dariole moulds which have been brushed with melted fat. The moulds should be about half full. Leave moulds in a warm place covered with a damp cloth for a further 20 minutes.

Set oven at 425F/220C/Gas Mark 7.

Bake the babas in the pre-heated oven for 10-15 minutes. Turn out from the moulds and leave on a wire rack to cool.

To make the syrup, put the water and sugar in a small saucepan and warm gradually while the sugar melts. Bring to the boil and cook briskly for about 5 minutes. Dip each baba in the syrup until it is well soaked with it. Arrange the soaked babas on a serving dish, spoon a little cream on the top of each one and place a strawberry on top. Arrange the remaining strawberries around the babas with any leftover syrup and serve immediately.

Confectionery

BLACKBERRY BALLS

4ozs/125g blackberries
2ozs/50g cake crumbs
1oz/25g castor sugar
A little icing sugar

Press the blackberries through a sieve and mix the purée with the cake crumbs and sugar. Form the mixture into balls and roll in the icing sugar. Delicious served with vanilla ice cream.

FROSTED CURRANTS

1 egg white
Castor sugar

Use black or redcurrants. Dip in the egg white and place on a plate. Sprinkle over the castor sugar and leave to set. Use for decorating a dessert or cake.

ARABIAN CURRANTS

1lb/500g almond paste
1lb/500g blackcurrants (with stalks removed)
4ozs/125g sugar
A little water

Line an shallow ovenproof dish with the almond paste with a raised edge. Cook the blackcurrants with the sugar and a little water until fruit is soft. Pour into the almond tart and bake for a 8-10 minutes in a moderate oven (350F/180C/Gas Mark 4). Serve cold.

BLACKBERRY JELLIES

2lbs/1kg blackberries (washed)
14ozs/440g granulated sugar
2tbsp/30ml melted butter
12fl.ozs/375ml liquid pectin
Castor sugar for coating

Line a 10"/25cm square cake tin with baking paper. Put the blackberries and half the sugar in a food processor and purée. Pass the purée through a fine sieve into a saucepan and add the remaining sugar. Bring the purée to the boil over a low heat, stirring continuously, and when boiling, cook for 2 minutes. Add the butter and continue stirring and boiling for another 2 minutes. Remove pan from heat and stir in the pectin. Pour into the prepared cake tin and leave to set in a cool place for 12 hours. Cut the jelly into required shapes and roll in the castor sugar. Store in a cool place in an airtight container, separating the layers of jellies, and they will keep for about a week.

CARAMELIZED STRAWBERRIES

4 1/2 ozs/140g sugar
5tbsp/75ml water
6ozs/175g good strawberries (washed and gently dried - do not remove hulls)

Put the sugar and water in a heavy-based saucepan and cook over a gentle heat until the sugar is dissolved, stirring occasionally. Bring to the boil and cook until the mixture becomes pale caramel in colour. Remove immediately from the heat and place in a bowl of warm water. Carefully dip the strawberries in the caramel and place on a lightly greased baking sheet or wire rack. Allow to cool and harden.
When ready to serve, place in paper sweet cases and use within 24 hours.

NB. Grapes, segmented tangerines, cherries, kumquats will also caramelise well.

STRAWBERRIES IN CHOCOLATE

20-25 good strawberries (washed and gently dried - do not remove hulls)
6ozs/175g plain chocolate
1/2 ounce/13g cooking fat

Break the chocolate into pieces and place in a bowl. Put the bowl in a saucepan of gently simmering water and gradually melt the chocolate with the cooking fat. Remove from heat. Take each strawberry carefully and dip in the melted chocolate and leave on a lightly greased sheet until set.
Serve in paper sweet cases and store in a covered jar in a refrigerator.

Index